LEGALIZING DRUGS

Other Books in the At Issue Series:

Affirmative Action
Business Ethics
Domestic Violence
Ethnic Conflict
Immigration Policy
The Media and Politics
Policing the Police
Rape on Campus
Smoking
What Is Sexual Harassment?
U.S. Policy Toward China

LEGALIZING DRUGS

David Bender, *Publisher*
Bruno Leone, *Executive Editor*
Scott Barbour, *Managing Editor*
Brenda Stalcup, *Series Editor*
Karin L. Swisher, *Book Editor*

An Opposing Viewpoi

Greenhaven Press, Inc
San Diego, California

Library of Congress Cataloging-in-Publication Data

Legalizing drugs / Karin L. Swisher, book editor.
p. cm. — (At issue) (An opposing viewpoints series)
Includes bibliographical references and index.
ISBN 1-56510-379-3 (alk. paper). — ISBN 1-56510-378-5 (pbk. : alk. paper).
1. Drug legalization—United States. 2. Drug abuse—United States. I. Swisher, Karin, 1966- . II. Series. III. Series: Opposing viewpoints series (Unnumbered)
HV5825.L437 1996
364.1'77'0973—dc20 95-24105
CIP

Printed in the U.S.A.

Table of Contents

Introduction

Since the 1960s, when the use of illegal drugs became more culturally acceptable, public policy experts in the United States have attempted to address several problems they believe result from the use and sale of drugs such as marijuana, cocaine, and heroin. One concern is the harm—physical, economic, and otherwise—that drug use may have on individuals, especially those who become addicted to hard-core drugs such as heroin or cocaine. Moreover, some experts contend that drug use by individuals is detrimental to society as a whole because it limits users' ability to function as responsible, productive members of their communities. Another area of concern is the criminal activity associated with both local drug sales and international trafficking. This problem became especially acute in the mid-1980s with the arrival of crack, a cheap smokable form of cocaine that swept America's inner cities and that is believed responsible for a sizable increase in gang activity and violence.

For three decades, federal, state, and local governments have attempted to address these issues—collectively referred to as "the drug problem"—by enforcing strict laws against the possession, use, and sale of illegal drugs. Referred to throughout the 1980s as the "war on drugs," this policy has continued into the 1990s.

Since the late 1980s, however, some have challenged the government's decision to use law enforcement to solve the drug problem in the United States. These commentators, who include libertarians, public policy experts, and health care professionals, argue that a new solution is necessary since the current one—strict law enforcement—is ineffective. They contend that such strict enforcement has had a negative effect on the drug situation. It has driven up drug prices significantly (some estimates place the profits of the illegal drug trade as high as $100 billion per year worldwide), inducing international drug cartels and urban street gangs alike to participate in high levels of drug trafficking. Both the cartels and street gangs are well-armed and commonly use assassinations to eliminate rivals and gain territory for drug sales. Although increasing amounts of funding have been devoted to law enforcement agencies and the criminal justice system, legalization advocates argue, it has had little effect on either drug trafficking and the accompanying violence or the availability and use of drugs on the street. They also contend that stringent enforcement of drug laws has labeled drug users and addicts as criminals, preventing many from seeking help out of fear of arrest and prosecution. According to Arnold S. Trebach, a professor in the department of justice, law, and society at the School of Public Affairs at The American University in Washington, D.C., "The urban situation in America is so desperate as to demand the nearly immediate dismantling of drug prohibition."

Proponents cite several benefits of drug legalization. First, they maintain that legalization would drastically reduce the profits associated with the illegal drug trade. International drug cartels and urban street gangs would, therefore, no longer be drawn to the high profits from the drug trade, they contend. Legalization, proponents argue, would eliminate the profit motive and put many of the cartels and street gangs out of business, leading to a reduction of the violence that results from international and local turf wars and assassinations. In addition, these advocates assert that legalization would clear overcrowded courts and jails because most of the hundreds of thousands of people arrested each year for drug possession and sale would no longer be entering the criminal justice system. Finally, they argue that the money saved in law enforcement and legal costs would provide a ready pool to support drug abuse prevention programs for children, to help urban teenagers find productive employment, and to fund the expensive treatment programs for addicts.

Opponents, however, argue that if currently illegal drugs were legalized, the drug problem would become immeasurably worse in a number of ways. Legalizing drugs, they contend, would increase the number of users by removing a primary barrier to drug use—laws. In addition, they argue, legalization would allow abusers to obtain drugs more cheaply and easily, causing more abusers to become addicts. More addicts would then exacerbate what Lee P. Brown calls the "human carnage" of drug use. In a speech given before the Massachusetts Civil Liberties Union, Brown argues that drug legalization would result in increased "addiction, drug-exposed infants, drug-induced accidents, loss of productivity, loss of employment, family breakdown and the degeneration of communities." New York columnist A.M. Rosenthal concurs: "The U.S. is still paying in broken lives, fear, violence and damaged newborns for the tacit decriminalization won by the counterculture in the 60's."

Legalizing drugs would be a complex, unprecedented, and potentially dangerous change in public policy. Some view legalization as a possible solution to some of the nation's deepest-seated problems. Others view legalization as a surrender in the war on drugs. The authors in *At Issue: Legalizing Drugs* debate which of these two views should guide the nation's efforts to solve the drug problem.

1

Drugs in America: An Overview

Close Up Foundation

The Close Up Foundation is an educational organization in Alexandria, Virginia, that encourages responsible participation in the democratic process.

Before the early years of the twentieth century, such drugs as heroin, cocaine, and marijuana were completely unregulated and were widely used in patent medicines. In 1906 the U.S. government passed the Pure Food and Drug Act, regulating many medicines for the first time by requiring accurate labels if they contained such drugs as cocaine or opium. Since then, laws dealing with these drugs have become more strict, eventually making their sale, possession, and use illegal. Many experts now argue that drug laws have caused the crime and violence that trouble American society and assert that many of the laws should thus be repealed—legalizing drugs. Other experts, however, contend that strict drug laws have successfully decreased drug use in the past and should continue to be enforced.

In 1982, President Ronald Reagan, concerned that illegal drug use was ruining the nation, declared an all-out war on drugs. Individuals and families were being devastated by drug addiction, and trade in illegal drugs was bringing unprecedented violence to cities. Drug-related crimes increased at a faster rate during the 1980s than any other type of crime. Many prisoners admitted committing crimes under the influence of drugs. Educators were concerned about drug deals taking place in or near their schools, and businesses reported that drug use was costing them $76 billion a year in decreased productivity.

The federal government spent $10 billion during the 1980s to fight illegal drugs. But in 1992 alone, spending for drug control jumped to $11.7 billion. Most of this money was spent to reduce drug supplies by expanding law enforcement programs and helping drug-exporting countries stem the flow of drugs to the United States. Some of the funds were earmarked for drug rehabilitation facilities and education programs.

Although the government has increased its spending on drug control, some Americans wonder whether the money is being used in the right way. They say that more money should be spent on preventive programs and less on law enforcement. Lawmakers continue to debate the best way to fight drugs. Should the government try to curb Americans' appetites for illegal drugs, or should it try to stop drugs from reaching the public by cracking down on drug dealers and producers?

Drug control in the United States

Narcotics in the nineteenth century. During the late 1800s, narcotics were sold freely, and many popular patent medicines contained narcotics. One of the most common drugs was cocaine, which was used in asthma remedies, toothache drops, and even soft drinks. By the turn of the century, the negative effects of cocaine on behavior and health were evident, and many states enacted laws to restrict its use. Some states also began drug education programs in their schools.

The first federal law to control cocaine use was the Pure Food and Drug Act of 1906, which required manufacturers of over-the-counter remedies to identify any cocaine content on their labels. In 1914, Congress passed the Harrison Act, the nation's first sweeping antinarcotics law. The act tightly regulated the legal sale and distribution of drugs and consequently drove the profitable drug trade into the hands of criminals.

Alcohol and Prohibition. In the early 1900s, pressure on federal lawmakers began to grow to ban alcohol production and sales. Organizations such as the Women's Christian Temperance Union and the Anti-Saloon League helped to convince members of Congress of the dangers of consuming alcohol. Temperance advocates claimed that working-class families were suffering because workers spent scarce wages and long hours drinking in saloons. They argued that drunkenness often led to violence. Employers, too, complained about workers who were absent, inefficient, or dangerous because they were drunk. And some people opposed alcohol on moral and religious grounds.

Finally, in 1917, Congress responded by passing a constitutional amendment prohibiting the production and sale of alcohol. The Eighteenth Amendment went into effect January 16, 1920.

Within a year it became obvious that Prohibition was not working. It was almost as easy for Americans to buy illegal alcohol after 1920 as it had been to acquire legal alcohol before the Eighteenth Amendment was passed. Government agents were unable to police the millions of Americans who made their own alcohol at home or purchased illegal alcohol from "bootleggers" who supplied it for high prices. In many cities, illegal saloons, known as "speakeasies," served liquor to customers.

The trade in illegal alcohol provided a new and profitable source of income for crime organizations. For example, Al Capone built a large criminal empire in Chicago based largely on supplying illegal alcohol. Capone guarded his businesses with armed gangsters who were willing to kill to protect their profits. Other regions had their own gangs, who often paid local officials not to arrest them for selling liquor.

By the 1930s, public sentiment to overturn Prohibition was growing.

Urban Americans, many of whom had opposed the Eighteenth Amendment from the beginning, deplored the violence and crime that Prohibition had brought to their cities. Others were convinced that the ban on alcohol was unenforceable. The Prohibition Bureau once estimated that its agents were catching only 5 percent of the liquor that was smuggled in from other countries. Finally, in 1933, the Eighteenth Amendment was repealed, and it was once again legal to make and drink alcoholic beverages. The next major government effort to control drug abuse did not occur until forty years later when recreational use of drugs became popular among the young.

Drugs and the counterculture. In the 1960s, young people began to grow more scornful of the values and conventions of middle-class America and began to create a new youth culture—or counterculture—which included rock music, freer attitudes toward sex, and drugs. The most common drug was marijuana, although LSD, a stronger hallucinogen; "speed," an amphetamine that produces increased nervous activity; and heroin also became popular.

In 1972, President Richard Nixon began government programs to end drug, and especially heroin, abuse. He declared a "total war against dangerous drugs" and vowed to stop foreign aid to countries that allowed drug traffickers to operate. In 1973, Nixon created the Drug Enforcement Administration to fight drug abuse.

The war on drugs

Reagan's efforts. During the 1980s, LSD and heroin use decreased while cocaine gained popularity. Cocaine has been called the drug of the '80s, and it was during that time that a new smokeable form called "crack" emerged. Because crack is highly addictive and inexpensive, it became popular with young and poor drug users. In 1982, President Ronald Reagan declared his all-out war on drugs. Reagan created a task force to prevent South American smugglers from importing cocaine into the country, and his wife, Nancy, launched her "Just Say No" campaign to encourage schoolchildren to say no to drug dealers.

President Reagan signed several antidrug laws passed by Congress during his presidency. In 1984, he approved anticrime legislation that allowed the government to seize the property of drug traffickers and authorized tougher penalties for drug-trafficking offenses. The Antidrug Abuse Act of 1986 stiffened penalties for drug traffickers and authorized more government money for law enforcement. A stricter antidrug act passed in 1988 created the Office of National Drug Control Policy to develop a national strategy to combat drug abuse. This act also imposed harsher penalties against drug offenders, including the denial of federal benefits for "recreational" users. Drug users could lose their eligibility for government student and housing loans, federal contracts, and any licenses or permits issued by the federal government.

The Bush strategy. In 1989, President George Bush announced a four-part plan to fight illegal drugs. The first part of the Bush strategy was to expand law enforcement and criminal justice measures to deal with drug offenses. He proposed expanding the number of prisons, courts, and prosecutors to make sure that drug dealers are arrested and punished. The president's 1993 budget allocated $15.8 billion for all law enforcement programs, including hiring more drug agents for the Drug Enforcement Administration and the Federal Bureau of Investigation, increasing the number of U.S. attorneys to prosecute drug crimes, and adding 4,200 spaces in federal penitentiaries.

Although the government has increased its spending on drug control, some Americans wonder whether the money is being used in the right way.

The second part of the Bush plan called on the United States to provide assistance to Bolivia, Colombia, Ecuador, and Peru—countries that produce most of the cocaine exported to the United States—to help them reduce production and trafficking of illegal drugs. In 1990, President Bush met with the leaders of these four countries at a drug summit in Colombia. At that meeting, the presidents stressed the need for South American farmers to be able to substitute legal crops such as coffee or flowers for the illegal coca leaf used to make cocaine. President Bush pledged to expand U.S. markets for legal substitute crops and proposed a five-year, $2.2 billion aid program for the region. The 1993 budget granted $768 million for the South American nations and Mexico as long as these nations show commitment to reducing narcotics production and respect for human rights. Part of the assistance calls for the United States to train local police forces in these countries to disrupt drug trafficking and destroy coca and to provide aircraft and boats for these efforts.

The third part of the president's strategy was to provide treatment to help addicts stop using drugs. The 1993 budget allocates $2.2 billion for treatment programs. Most of this money goes to state-sponsored treatment programs and allows 49,000 more users to participate than could under the 1992 budget. Some of the treatment funds finance research about the nature and treatment of addictive disorders and special programs for addicted prisoners and pregnant women.

The last part of the Bush strategy was to fund drug education programs that seek to prevent children from becoming drug users, that encourage current users to quit, and that discourage users from progressing to more dangerous drugs or practices. In 1992, the government spent $1.5 billion on prevention efforts that include mass media campaigns, school-based drug education, and community programs. The total cost of the war on drugs for 1992 was $11.7 billion, an 11 percent increase over 1991.

Drug strategies

In recent years, the federal government has increased funding to fight drugs. Although members of Congress agree that illegal drugs are a problem, they disagree on how the government should spend its money fighting drugs. Currently, about 70 percent of the drug budget is used to reduce drug supplies, and 30 percent is used to reduce demand through prevention and treatment programs.

Some policymakers believe that the government should continue to use most of the funds to limit the supply of drugs. They want government agencies to hire more customs agents and border patrol officers to prevent drugs from entering the country and more police officers to arrest drug dealers. Some members of Congress have proposed using the military to inspect ships suspected of transporting cocaine or marijuana to the United States. They support U.S.-sponsored programs that train foreign police officers to catch drug traffickers and that pay local farmers to grow new crops to replace those used to make illegal drugs.

Other officials say that the real problem is the demand for illegal drugs in the United States, and that more money should be spent on education, treatment, and antipoverty programs. They want the government to focus more on drug users, claiming that drug producers, traffickers, and dealers will continue to operate as long as Americans are willing to buy drugs. They argue that the government should use its money to help users by funding treatment programs and educating Americans, particularly youth, about the dangers of drugs. Many experts claim that government drug policies do not address the roots of drug abuse, such as poverty, illiteracy, and unemployment. They maintain that drug use would decrease if the government spent more money to solve the underlying problems that cause people to use illegal drugs in the first place.

By the turn of the century, the negative effects of cocaine on behavior and health were evident, and many states enacted laws to restrict its use.

Drug testing. As part of the war on drugs, forty-five government agencies require job applicants to submit to drug testing, and some departments randomly test their employees for drug use. And departments that do test often claim success. For example, the military has reported that drug testing greatly contributed to an 82 percent decline in drug use from 1981 to 1989, and the Department of Transportation also reported a decline in the percentage of employees testing positive for illegal drugs. However, dozens of unions and workers' groups have filed lawsuits against drug testing programs, and some have won their cases in court. Nevertheless, federal officials hope that private businesses will follow the government's lead and adopt similar measures. According to the Bureau of Labor Statistics, the percentage of employers with formal drug abuse policies has increased by more than 60 percent.

Proponents of drug testing claim that drug abuse decreases worker productivity and increases absenteeism, costing companies millions of dollars every year. Therefore, drug abusers need to be weeded out. In addition, supporters point out that society cannot tolerate drug abuse in certain occupational areas such as public transportation or nuclear power. Advocates of drug testing believe that the danger to society is too great to continue giving individuals the freedom to abuse drugs.

However, drug testing raises serious questions about the right of employers to control the private behavior of their workers. Many civil liberties groups view random drug testing as a violation of the Fourth Amendment, which prohibits unreasonable search and seizure. They say that a worker has an inalienable right to privacy and should be free from unwarranted harassment. In addition, drug testing opponents claim that such tests are often inaccurate, distorted by some foods and medicines, and may thereby jeopardize the careers of innocent workers.

Legalization. Despite the billions of dollars spent on combating drugs, illegal substances still enter the United States, where users are often prepared to pay high prices for them. Some public officials and other citizens say that current drug policies have failed and that the United States should decriminalize illegal drugs. Supporters of legalization contend that current drug laws have brought about conditions similar to Prohibition in the 1920s. They cite the huge profits traffickers make from sales and the violence that competition among dealers has brought to the nation's cities. Advocates of legalization argue that if the government permitted drugs, illegal drugs would become less expensive and more easily available, thereby eliminating profitability for the drug traffickers. Thus, drug traffickers would go out of business, and much of the violence would cease.

Americans who favor legalization also argue that if drugs were decriminalized, the government would be able to set standards for cocaine, heroin, and marijuana in the same ways that it now controls alcohol and other drugs. Government officials could decide the strength of drugs, assure that they were free from other harmful chemicals, and prohibit their sale to minors. Legalization advocates maintain that if the government treated current illegal drugs as it now treats alcohol, it could allow drug sales, and, at the same time, discourage new users through education about the effects of abuse. A portion of the money needed for education programs could come from taxes on the drugs themselves. Some say that, like alcohol, drugs can have recreational uses and that not all who use them will become addicted. Proponents of legalization contend that although less expensive legal drugs may cause more people to experiment with or use them, most people will not become addicted, and that if they understand the dangers, most will still choose to avoid them.

Although members of Congress agree that illegal drugs are a problem, they disagree on how the government should spend its money fighting drugs.

Many other Americans do not like the idea of making drugs legal. They believe that drugs should remain illegal and that the government should continue its fight against them. This group argues that making drugs legal would tell people that drug use is socially acceptable and safe, even though it can result in health problems and death. They say that less expensive, legal drugs will cause more people to use them because they will no longer fear arrest and will be able to afford the lower costs. Opponents of legalization also contend that legalization will result in more addicted Americans, who will be dangerous to themselves and others around them and who will require increased spending for drug treatment programs.

Those who believe in keeping drugs illegal point out that when narcotics laws were tightened beginning in 1914, drug use declined until the

1960s when it again became acceptable. They believe that a similar stiffening of the laws and an emphasis on enforcing them will again lower drug abuse. Critics of legalization are also skeptical of the idea that criminal activity will be reduced if drugs are permissible. They point to Great Britain, where heroin is legally available from designated clinics for certified addicts yet is still sold illegally on the black market. These skeptics believe that current U.S. laws should not be changed simply because some Americans are not deterred by them.

A long-term view

Spending for the war on drugs increased from $1.1 billion in 1981 to $11.7 billion in 1992. Most of this money went for law enforcement to reduce the supply of drugs. Some Americans believe that this strategy works. They point to recent surveys showing that the number of drug users has declined from 23 million in 1985 to 12.9 million in 1990. During that time, the number of cocaine users fell from 5.8 million to 1.6 million, although some studies in 1991 indicated that cocaine use was beginning to rise again. However, others think that drug use would drop faster if more money were spent on treatment, education, and social programs. And still other people advocate decriminalizing illegal drugs. As long as drugs continue to pour into the United States and Americans continue to use them, presidents and lawmakers will debate which strategy will best protect the United States from the ravages of drug abuse.

2
Drugs Should Be Legalized

Doug Bandow

Doug Bandow is a senior fellow at the Cato Institute—a libertarian think tank—and a nationally syndicated columnist with the Copley News Service.

The criminalization of drug use is counterproductive for the following reasons: It violates people's individual rights; it fails to reduce drug use; and it results in the creation of a black market, posing dangers to users and children and causing crime. The United States should legalize drugs and regulate them in a manner similar to the way cigarettes are controlled.

Although hostilities abroad captured the attention of Americans [as the 1991 Persian Gulf War played out], the U.S. remained mired in a costly domestic conflict—the drug war. While both President Bush and members of Congress seemed to hope the issue would simply fade away, millions of people still used drugs, drug-related crime and killings continued to rise in major cities, drug enforcement officials violated the civil liberties of the innocent as well as the guilty, and drug dealers seduced young people into joining their criminal enterprises.

Yet as the drug war has dragged on, the sense of crisis that once surrounded it has lessened—making this an opportune moment to reassess the war and debate the direction of future policy. For we must consider more than the usual minor reforms advanced by Washington policy makers. We need, instead, a serious and rational debate on the legalization, or really re-legalization, of drugs.

Proposals for legalizing drugs have entered the mainstream of public debate in recent years. Frustration with a futile, yet ever more costly war on drugs has prompted support for legalization from a number of respected, conservative figures, such as Milton Friedman and William F. Buckley, Jr., as well as present and past public officials, such as Baltimore Mayor Kurt Schmoke, former Secretary of State George Shultz, and federal Judge Robert Sweet. Some people, like William Bennett, the former drug czar, have denounced "intellectuals" for even raising legalization as an option. Privately, however, many of those on the front lines, including cops, prosecutors, and pastors, now want to end drug prohibition.

Yet what would legalization really mean? Some advocates of the status quo have found it easier to criticize the absence of a blueprint for legalization than to defend drug prohibition, as if the lack of detailed consensus among legalization advocates justified the excesses of the drug war. Writing in the *Public Interest*, James Jacobs, a professor at New York University Law School, argued, "The lack of a fleshed-out legalization proposal makes it extremely difficult to assess or to criticize the legalization position. Skeptics vainly try to fix their sights on a moving target." In the interest of putting such criticism to rest, I want to spell out here how legalization might work in practice.

Why legalization?

Criminal sanctions against drug use are bad policy for at least five reasons:

- Criminal sanctions against drug use improperly limit the freedom of adults to use substances no more dangerous than others now available legally and imprison people for actions that do not directly harm others, in contrast to most crimes.
- Criminalizing drug use fails to reduce it significantly. A large percentage of the population has experimented with drugs (one-third of those over the age of twelve have used marijuana, for instance). Most others have access to drugs if they want.
- Sanctions increase the danger of drug use by forcing users into an illicit market.
- Criminalizing drugs entices children to use and sell drugs by creating a criminal underground offering kids economic opportunities unavailable elsewhere.
- Drug prohibition causes the bulk of murders and property crime in major urban areas by creating a black market characterized by warring suppliers, who charge inflated prices to users, who in turn steal to pay for their habits. Drug prohibition also fosters crime abroad, funding violent entrepreneurs and even terrorist insurgencies that threaten fragile civilian governments in poor countries.

The repeal of drug prohibition would, of course, not result in heaven on earth, but it would allow a reduction in spending on the criminal justice system, end the steady increase in arrests and imprisonments, cut the number of deaths from drug use, reduce the temptation posed to children, and cut the crime rate. Overall, drug use would likely rise, but probably only modestly; the increase would consist chiefly of casual experimentation, which is not a serious problem in the absence of criminal sanctions and an illegal market. Although the mere elimination of criminal penalties for drug use would cause some combination of these effects, the exact impact on crime and drug use would depend upon how drugs were legalized.

Legalization options

The question of what would follow the end of drug prohibition is thus vitally important. "Even if a legalization option were adopted," says one outspoken opponent, Congressman Charles Rangel (D-NY), "many questions remain as to how drug usage would be regulated." But, he complains, advocates of legalization "never seem to have answers."

Dropping the ban on drug use would not be a jump into the unknown. The United States has long experience regulating alcohol and tobacco and for more than a century allowed the use of cocaine, marijuana, and opium. Moreover, many other nations, such as the Netherlands and Great Britain, eschew America's draconian prohibitionist policies. Marijuana is effectively legal in the Netherlands, while in Britain doctors are able to prescribe not only heroin, but in an experimental program in Liverpool also smokable (though not crack) cocaine.

Because virtually no legalization advocate proposes unrestricted drug sale and use, there are a number of strategies for creating a legal market. These include six major options:

- legalize the less dangerous drugs;
- decriminalize, rather than fully legalize drugs;
- require use through a doctor;
- sell drugs in government stores, as alcohol is sold in some states;
- allow the sale of drugs in private establishments, with some restrictions, such as bans on sales to minors and the use of vending machines;
- permit unrestricted sales.

Since each alternative has somewhat different advantages and drawbacks, we need to give separate attention to each one.

The least radical step to relax drug prohibition would be to differentiate types of drugs, legalizing those viewed as least dangerous. Not surprisingly, marijuana receives the widest support for legalization, although some analysts would add heroin. Stephen Mugford, an Australian sociologist, has suggested distinguishing between cannabis, on the one hand, and cocaine and heroin, on the other, by making the former available commercially and the latter only through a licensing system.

Many of those on the front lines, including cops, prosecutors, and pastors, now want to end drug prohibition.

Partial legalization would eliminate some of the worst features of prohibition by dropping sanctions from the most widely used illicit substance or substances. Legalizing marijuana alone would end half or more of all current drug arrests, well over one million a year, allowing either a reduction in enforcement efforts or a concentration on the sale of harder drugs. Doing so would also cut out an important profit center for criminal dealers.

Moreover, allowing the legal use of pot would help provide a firebreak between use of the most acceptable illegal drug and use of other, "harder" drugs. In contrast to today's illicit providers, legal dealers offering marijuana would have no incentive to move customers on to amphetamines, cocaine, or heroin. Users would also more likely distinguish between a substance viewed as comparatively benign and other drugs that the government was still attempting to keep out of their hands. Dr. Giel van Brussell, head of the Narcotics Office of Amsterdam's Department of Health, cites this as a major factor in the success of his country's policies: Young people can buy marijuana "in the coffee shops and see that it's relatively harmless. They can also see that hard-drug users suffer from physical deterioration." To enforce criminal penalties against both groups, he argues, would merge the two now very different drug scenes.

This approach would also offer the opportunity to expand the policy after further study. Ethan Nadelmann, a professor at Princeton's Woodrow Wilson School, suggests a gradual "shift toward legalization" beginning with the legalization of marijuana, which would provide "ample opportunity to halt, reevaluate, and redirect drug policies that begin to prove too costly or counterproductive."

Nevertheless, maintaining the drug war, even while reducing its scope, would perpetuate many current problems. If heroin remained illegal, property crime would remain high as addicts continued to steal to finance their habits. Keeping crack illegal would ensure continued violence as dealers fought over territory. Even if the government concentrated on controlling these substances, it would not be able to eradicate their sale, at least not at an acceptable cost. For instance, one briefcase of synthetic heroin could supply all of New York's addicts for a year. America will never be able to eliminate the distribution of so little product between willing sellers and buyers and remain a free society. Nor will foreign nations be free of violence and terror as long as cocaine and heroin are produced in their countries by criminal cartels.

A policy of partial prohibition would also maintain the morally questionable practice of locking up people who do no direct harm to others. It would still drive what is primarily a health and social problem underground, creating a stigma that makes it difficult for some people to get help. And it would discourage medical research and information dissemination about the dangers of drug use.

Decriminalization

Another option would be to decriminalize, rather than fully legalize, drugs. The government could substitute civil for criminal sanctions against drug use, punishing users with a fine rather than prison; at the same time the government would maintain criminal penalties against sellers, as did the eleven states that decriminalized marijuana use in the 1970s. (This was, in fact, essentially the law during Prohibition.)

Decriminalization would preserve legal disapproval of drug use, thereby presumably discouraging demand to some degree, without jailing people for harming themselves. Enforcement efforts could be relaxed and prison resources reduced.

Still, decriminalization would not fully address the problems that make legalization the best option. While users would not go to jail, those who were caught would be punished for committing an act not unlike pouring a drink. Moreover, the government would still arrest and imprison those who supplied an arbitrary set of substances to willing buyers.

As a result, the black market would remain a profitable field for criminals, leaving largely unchanged the problems of corruption, crime, and violence that exist today. And by keeping drug use illicit if not criminal, decriminalization would still discourage drug research and information-sharing, prevent any quality control or dosage standardization for drug use, and leave kids vulnerable to the allure of the drug trade.

Physician approval

Some support exists for a third alternative: requiring the approval of a physician to use drugs, as under the British system. Drug use would be legal, but drugs would be available only through a doctor, who would either provide a prescription or dispense the drugs. In 1989, for instance, New York state senator Joseph Galiber introduced legislation allowing licensed doctors and pharmacists to sell drugs (without requiring prescriptions). A related approach, advanced by attorney Frederick Campbell, would be to limit the availability of drugs to recognized addicts through special clinics. Or the government could require licensure for legal users. For instance, Mark Kleiman of Harvard University has suggested creating a "drinking license" that could be revoked if abused.

The advantage of these sort of systems is that they would retain some controls over users, who might have to sit through a lecture on the health effects of their preferred drug, be continually monitored by a doctor, and so on. The system would also preserve some stigma for users, presumably discouraging demand.

Unfortunately, the very benefits of the system would also cause its biggest drawbacks. By placing users under the control of doctors, the system would degrade consumers. Such a process seems unfair—why pot smokers but not cigarette smokers? Also, the more stringent the system, the more likely that an illicit market would continue. If addicts alone received drugs, there would still be widespread demand for black market supplies from those not designated as addicts. Moreover, some people would attempt to be recognized as addicts to become eligible to receive drugs; addiction would, in Kleiman's words, be "a legally privileged status."

The experience of Great Britain demonstrates the problems of this system. A small number of doctors with a special license may prescribe cocaine, dipipanone (a powerful narcotic), and heroin. They may also determine how the addict satisfies his habit—with oral doses of methadone, for instance, rather than injections. The stringency of the system, especially after the government tightened its rules in 1968, has sharply limited users' legal access to drugs. As a result, crime has increased as more users attempt to circumvent what they consider to be a humiliating rule.

The repeal of drug prohibition would . . . allow a reduction in spending on the criminal justice system.

The resulting black market is not nearly as severe as in the U.S., with far less crime, as well as fewer deaths from AIDS passed among intravenous drug users. However, only about 7,000 of an estimated 30,000 to 35,000 heroin addicts were purchasing drugs legally in 1985. Leaving a similar 80 percent of cocaine, crack, heroin, and marijuana users outside of the legal market in the U.S. would ensure the survival of a huge, violent criminal underground.

Even a system allowing almost anyone to use drugs but only at a clinic would not eliminate black market demand. Such a system, observes Nancy Lord, an attorney and doctor, would "not be attractive to addicts who use drugs in a home environment, with their choice of friends, music and food. The prospect of restricting their drug use to a clinical or governmental setting would probably be so unattractive to them that the demand for black market drugs would undoubtedly continue."

Finally, such a system would place an inappropriate burden on doctors. Many who view their job as healing the sick would be uncomfortable dispensing potentially dangerous drugs, even to willing users. And throwing the drug problem into physicians' offices is probably not a good use of medical resources, especially given the current problem of providing Americans with affordable care.

Government stores for drugs

Another form of legalization would be to sell drugs in government stores, as alcohol is sold in some states. When Prohibition was ended by the Twenty-First Amendment, the law did more than just return to the status quo. Instead, the Twenty-First Amendment both repealed the Eighteenth Amendment, which had made the manufacture, sale, and transportation of alcohol illegal, and gave states almost carte blanche over alcohol use within their borders.

Alcohol regulation across the country is a patchwork. Most states allow the sale of beer and wine in private stores, but some limit hard liquor sales to state "ABC" stores. Some give counties authority to ban sales by the drink in bars. The drinking age once varied by state, although federal pressure—including the threat to cut off highway funds—has prompted every state to increase the age to twenty-one. Alcohol is widely advertised, but state stores do not promote their wares in this way.

Thus, currently illicit drugs could be made available to adults in state stores. The government would merely be in charge of selling, not growing or making drugs, which could come from domestic or foreign sources. The latter markets would likely become legal once the U.S. stopped pressuring foreign nations to disrupt their societies by following Washington's prohibitionist policies. There would be no advertising (courts have ruled that government may place more restrictions on "commercial" speech than on other forms). Prices would reflect a component to help pay for the social cost of drug use.

Such an approach would be a vast improvement over prohibition, eliminating the black market and the vast profits made by criminal enterprises. A gray market serving the young would still exist, but such "leakage" would pose less of a problem than we have today. Because illegal sales would largely disappear, children would not likely be recruited as dealers of drugs. (No high school students wear beepers selling alcohol or cigarettes, despite the leakage in those markets.)

One problem of government-controlled distribution is that it might appear to give an official imprimatur to drug use. Opponents of legalization have long argued that eliminating the legal prohibition on drug use would appear to encourage drug use. Yet unenforceable legal prohibitions have had little apparent effect in shaping moral attitudes. Nevertheless, having the government provide and profit from sales may appear to sanction use. Indeed, Michael Gazzaniga, professor of neuroscience at Dartmouth Medical School, cautions against a plan that makes the government a pusher. "If the drug-treatment centers were dependent on income from the [government-run] Drugstore, the bureaucrats running the store might be tempted to increase profits."

Putting sales in the hands of a government monopoly would also eliminate the traditional benefits of competition for users. Prices would likely be higher, access more restricted, and service poorer in a government-controlled system. Of course, since even most advocates of legalization want to restrain use, just without resort to the criminal law, such inefficiency might be considered a benefit—unless it was so great as to make a black market a profitable option. Restraints on demand could, however, be better achieved by taxes on private sales. It would also be easier to adjust the tax to ensure that no black market flourishes.

Private drug sales

Another legalization option would be to allow the sale of drugs in private establishments, with some restrictions, such as a ban on sales to minors and the use of vending machines, as is done with cigarettes.

The most obvious benefit of following a "cigarette model" would be to eliminate the primary costs of prohibition: more than one million arrests annually, rampant crime, pervasive corruption, a violent criminal underground, and foreign terrorism. The substances sold would themselves be safer, since quality and quantity would be standardized, manufacturers would be liable for impurities, and information would be widely available about the health effects of different substances, at varying dosages and when used with other drugs. This approach would also be more appropriate for our form of free society, with a minimum of government control.

There are two major drawbacks to this approach. The first is that demand would probably increase to some degree. There are, however, reasons to believe that allowing the private sale of drugs would not turn the nation into a large crack house. For instance, we appear to have had no more opium addicts per capita when its use was legal than we have heroin addicts per capita today. Moreover, drug use responds to many factors, as does consumption of such substances as alcohol and tobacco, both of which have been falling even though they are cheap and legal.

In any case, the government could take steps to temper demand without being so draconian as to recreate a black market. Drugs could be taxed, generating revenue to help meet the cost imposed by drug users on society. Moreover, all advertising, including sponsorship of sporting events, could be banned, just as federal law currently forbids television advertising for cigarettes and distilled spirits. Moves currently underway at both the state and national levels would ban tobacco company sponsorship of athletic events and prohibit alcohol advertisements that suggest drinking a particular brand can improve one's social status. Georgette Bennett, a sociologist, has even proposed that drugs be sold generically, without any brand-name competition. (For similar reasons nationalization of the tobacco industry has been suggested.) Such a policy could be considered a variant of the government-stores approach.

The second major problem involves young people, who would undoubtedly get drugs, just as they are able to acquire cigarettes and liquor. No system would be foolproof; indeed, as of 1990, despite the expenditure of more than $10 billion annually, the federal government has not been able to prevent 22.7 percent of kids between ages twelve and seventeen from having tried illicit substances. (It is noteworthy that this number, which peaked at an incredible 34.3 percent in 1979, started to slide before the Reagan administration inaugurated its intensified drug war.) However, this form of legalization would allow the remaining drug enforcement efforts to be directed at limiting the "gray market" for the young. Drug vending machines also could be outlawed (just as many localities are now moving to ban cigarette machines) and merchants made liable for significant penalties for selling to young people. The problem of older friends and strangers buying drugs for young people, the principal means of minors' access to alcohol today, would remain, although more adults would probably view drug sales to kids as "wrong," helping to restrict access.

Unrestricted drug sales

Finally, the most drastic alternative would be to repeal the drug laws in their entirety, allowing unrestricted sales. All restrictions, other than tort liability for adulterated products, on currently illicit drugs could be lifted. Advocates of this position are in a minority, but include Ron Paul, formerly a Texas congressman. Drugs would be treated like aspirin, with virtually no restrictions on sales. Use by children would probably, though not necessarily, be prohibited; five states do not bar cigarette sales to minors. People using drugs would be held legally responsible for their actions, as are drunk drivers today.

The main practical benefit of such an approach is that it would eliminate the evils of prohibition. The advantage of this system compared to more regulated regimes is that it would avoid the costs and inefficiencies of government control and would not encourage the existence of any black or perhaps even gray market. Finally, it would maximize individual freedom, an important consideration usually overlooked in drug policy debates.

Nevertheless, the costs of this strategy might be significant. Children would certainly have greater access to drugs, yet there is a substantial interest in protecting them until they are considered legally competent to decide whether to use dangerous substances. Moreover, drug use could increase, perhaps sharply, imposing costs on other members of society, such as increased health care for indigent users. Such a result is not inevitable. Cocaine use was legal in the nineteenth and early twentieth century, and there is no evidence of a crisis at that time. Nevertheless, given the risks posed by widespread use of drugs, it is reasonable to try to discourage drug use and to collect revenue from users to help defray the social costs they generate.

A tentative proposal

Drug prohibition has failed. It is not just; imprisoning people for using a substance, even a harmful one, violates their basic rights unless their actions directly harm others. Yet most of the damage from drugs today results, not from their use, but from the ban on their use. Moreover, our reliance on criminal sanctions has not significantly reduced demand at an acceptable price, in terms of human freedom, deaths and crime, social disruption, and financial cost.

Since drug use is not harmless, however, some restrictions are appropriate. Mark Kleiman argues, "Our central concern should thus be with classes of users for whom the damage done by the drug is disproportionately higher: the young, the poor, and the heaviest users, and with the illicit market whose corruption, crime, violence and criminal income cause widespread damage."

What, then, should a legal market look like? Use by adults should be legal; criminal penalties should apply only to those who sell to youngsters. The Drug Enforcement Administration should be disbanded, with enforcement entrusted to local police, since sale to minors (rather than production or smuggling) would be the primary drug crime. Public pressure, too, could be brought to bear on firms to combat juvenile drug use; in late 1990, for example, the tobacco industry finally announced a campaign to curb smoking by minors.

Unenforceable legal prohibitions have had little apparent effect in shaping moral attitudes.

The federal government should prohibit advertising in any national or interstate medium and ban interstate sales by mail. All federal laws controlling distribution and sale should be repealed, however, leaving the issue up to the individual states. Thus, local and state governments could experiment with different systems.

Of particular interest should be a modified cigarette model. States would legalize the sale of all illicit substances, however damaging to the user. "While there are some drugs that we cringe at making legal," writes James Ostrowski, "these are the very drugs that the public would cringe at using if they were legalized."

Keeping these drugs illegal would merely increase the social costs associated with them. The only exception should be substances shown to cause a very high percentage of users to commit violent acts against others (perhaps PCP, for instance). The mere fact that users might be more likely to commit a crime—as are those who drink—would not be enough to warrant a ban. But users of legal drugs would be both civilly and criminally liable for actions they commit while under the influence. Driving offenses, for instance, would be treated like standard cases of drunk driving.

Private firms would be allowed to sell formerly illicit drugs, but such establishments would have to be specially licensed and regulated to limit leakage to children. Moreover, use of vending machines would be prohibited. As Ethan Nadelmann has noted: "It is important to realize that legalization does not have to mean following in the same stupid footsteps traced by our alcohol and tobacco policies. We do not have to make potentially dangerous substances available in vending machines at seven cents a piece in packages of 20. Nor do we have to subsidize growers or provide the substances at subsidized rates to our military personnel."

Advertising might be banned; warnings would be included on packaging and health information made available in stores. State governments would also prohibit public giveaways (a marketing ploy now used by some cigarette producers).

Manufacturers and sellers would bear normal tort liability for contaminated or mislabeled products, but users would assume the risk for using otherwise "safe" drugs. Developers of new drugs, however, might be held normally liable for any ill health effects of their products. The Food and Drug Administration could underwrite testing programs to measure the effects of different drugs, as well as determine what dosages are most safe. It would not be empowered to ban these sort of substances that it found to be dangerous, however, since that would move us back to prohibition. Retail outlets might face liability for selling to intoxicated patrons (through the so-called "dram shop" laws now applicable to bars, for instance) and could be closed as public nuisances if they created unreasonable disturbances in a neighborhood.

States could levy a tax on drug sales to finance an advertising and educational campaign on the substances' dangers, fund health care and addiction treatment programs for indigent users, and provide social services for the families of users who are harmed (just as some families fall into poverty because of the actions of alcoholics or chronic gamblers). Special consideration should be given to the use of drugs by pregnant women. Perhaps sale to anyone who is obviously pregnant should be banned; perhaps putative mothers who use drugs (including alcohol and tobacco) should face charges of child abuse. At the extreme, pregnant women who use drugs could be jailed, as have a handful in the past after positive drug tests. Such an extension of government control rests on questionable legal grounds as long as women are free to abort their pregnancies; moreover, such intrusive regulation is disturbing and difficult to enforce. But the consequences of drug use, like heavy alcohol consumption, during pregnancy do affect another human being who deserves protection by the state. Exactly what steps are appropriate requires further debate.

Most of the damage from drugs today results, not from their use, but from the ban on their use.

Finally, government officials should emphasize the role of the family, church, community, and business in restraining otherwise destructive behavior. Social pressure has helped reduce the appeal of alcohol and cigarettes; a growing majority of people support discouraging cigarette use in public places. Even illicit drug users respond to social pressure. For instance, Stephen Mugford found that cocaine users "limited their use, and did so because of the wider web of social ties into which they were embedded." Churches should speak to the more fundamental needs that cause people to seek solace in drugs. Private firms and public agencies, such as the Pentagon, could bar or limit drug use when it adversely affects productivity and safety. Government officials could also continue to use their "bully pulpit" to help harness various social forces to discourage irresponsible drug use after criminal sanctions were lifted. Indeed, it was just such pressure from Health and Human Services Secretary Louis Sullivan and other members of the black community that helped sink cigarette company plans to market new brands to blacks and women.

Overall, it is important to build a social ethic to discourage irresponsible behavior, whatever the drug involved. And that is only likely to come when people have choices. As Mark Kleiman has pointed out, coercion is hardly likely to improve anyone's power of self-control. Of course, legalization in itself would not promote self-control over destructive impulses. We need a concentrated effort by a whole range of social institutions to achieve that end.

A modified cigarette model appears to be the best intermediate position between prohibition and full legalization.

Many advocates of continued prohibition do not even want to discuss legalization. James Jacobs argues, "Perhaps the most negative effect of [the legalization] debate is that it is diverting time, resources, and attention from the more pressing question of how to reform the war on drugs so as to reduce drug use more effectively, and to minimize social and economic costs while preserving civil liberties." Yet that is precisely what the argument over legalization is about—deciding whether another strategy would better restrain drug use at far less social cost. Whether drug prohibition works does not depend on the method of legalization.

Still, if policy makers move toward legalization, the kind of system to be established will become an important issue. Spelling out legalization in practice may help satisfy some critics. But, as Nadelmann writes, "It is, in the final analysis, unreasonable to expect all advocates of what has been called 'legalization' to unite on a single plan. Like the 'drug prohibitionists,' they are split among themselves on moral, ideological, and political questions and vary greatly with respect to both their reassessments of the costs and benefits of alternative policies and their recommendations of which policies should be implemented."

In the end, we need to treat drugs as "a category of grudgingly tolerated vices," as an opponent of full legalization, Mark Kleiman, puts it. A modified cigarette model appears to be the best intermediate position between prohibition and full legalization. In adopting this approach we would simultaneously recognize the importance of individual rights by allowing adults to use currently banned substances and the importance of protecting others from irresponsible behavior by imposing reasonable restrictions on use and holding users responsible for any harm they cause. Such a system would best maximize individual freedom while minimizing the social costs of drug use.

3
Drug Prohibition Is Harmful

Barbara Ehrenreich

Barbara Ehrenreich is a well-known writer who contributes to such journals as Time *and* Z Magazine.

The federal government, in its zeal to eliminate drugs and drug use, has squandered billions of dollars on stringent law enforcement programs. This prohibition of drugs has made the drug trade highly lucrative, allowing organized crime—both the Mafia and street gangs—to flourish and the nation's murder rates to skyrocket. Harmful drug law enforcement efforts should therefore be abandoned in favor of decriminalization or legalization.

An evil grips America, a life-sapping, drug-related habit. It beclouds reason and corrodes the spirit. It undermines authority and nourishes a low-minded culture of winks and smirks. It's the habit of drug prohibition, and it's quietly siphoning off the resources that might be better used for drug treatment or prevention. Numerous authorities have tried to warn us, including most recently the Surgeon General, but she got brushed off like a piece of lint. After all, drug prohibition is right up there with heroin and nicotine among the habits that are hell to kick.

Admittedly, legalization wouldn't be problem-free either. Americans have a peculiarly voracious appetite for drugs, and probably no one should weigh in on the debate who hasn't seen a friend or loved one hollowed out by cocaine or reduced to selling used appliances on the street. But if drugs take a ghastly toll, drug prohibition has proved itself, year after year, to be an even more debilitating social toxin.

Consider the moral effects of marijuana prohibition. After booze and NyQuil, pot is probably America's No. 1 drug of choice—a transient, introspective high that can cure nausea or make the evening sitcoms look like devastating wit. An estimated 40 million Americans have tried it at some point, from Ivy League law professors to country-and-western singers. Yet in some states, possession of a few grams can get you put away for years. What does it do to one's immortal soul to puff and wink and look away while about 100,000 other Americans remain locked up for doing the exact same thing? Marijuana prohibition establishes a minimum baseline level of cultural dishonesty that we can never rise above: the President "didn't inhale," heh heh. It's O.K. to drink till you puke, but you mustn't ever smoke the vile weed, heh heh. One of the hardest things a parent can ever tell a bright and questioning teenager—after all the relevant sermonizing, of course—is, Well, just don't get caught.

Prohibition and organized crime

But the prohibition of cocaine and heroin may be more corrosive still. Here's where organized crime comes in, the cartels and kingpins and Crips and Bloods. These are the principal beneficiaries of drug prohibition; without it they'd be reduced to three-card monte and numbers scams. Legitimate entrepreneurs must sigh and shake their heads in envy: if only the government would ban some substance like Wheat Chex, for example, so it could be marketed for hundreds of dollars an ounce.

Yes, legal drugs, even if heavily taxed and extensively regulated, would no doubt be cheaper than illegal ones, which could mean more people sampling them out of curiosity. But this danger has to be weighed against the insidious marketing dynamic of illegal drugs, whose wildly inflated prices compel the low-income user to become a pusher and recruiter of new users.

Drugs can kill, of course. But drug prohibition kills too. In Washington, an estimated 80% of homicides are drug related, meaning drug-prohibition related. It's gunshot wounds that fill our urban emergency rooms, not ODs and bad trips. Then there's the perverse financial logic of prohibition. The billions we spend a year on drug-related law enforcement represent money not spent on improving schools and rebuilding neighborhoods. Those who can't hope for the lasting highs of achievement and self-respect are all too often condemned to crack.

So why don't we kick the prohibition habit? Is it high-minded puritanism that holds us back, or political cowardice? Or maybe it's time to admit that we cling to prohibition for the same reason we cling to so many other self-destructive habits: because we like the way they make us feel. Prohibition, for example, tends to make its advocates feel powerfully righteous, and militant righteousness has effects not unlike some demon mix of liquor and amphetamines: the eyes bulge, the veins distend, the voice begins to bray.

If drugs take a ghastly toll, drug prohibition has proved itself, year after year, to be an even more debilitating social toxin.

But the most seductive thing about prohibition is that it keeps us from having to confront all the other little addictions that get us through the day. It's the NutraSweet in the coffee we use to wash down the chocolate mousse; a dad's "Just say no" commandments borne on martini-scented breath. "Don't do drugs," a Members Only ad advises. "Do clothes." Well, why "do" anything? Why not live more lightly, without compulsions of any kind? Then there's TV, the addiction whose name we can hardly speak—the poor man's virtual reality, the substance-free citizen's 24-hour-a-day hallucinatory trip. No bleary-eyed tube addict, emerging from weekend-long catatonia, has the right to inveigh against "drugs."

When cornered, the prohibition addict has one last line of defense. We can't surrender in this war, he or she insists, because we'd be sending the "wrong message." But the message we're sending now is this: Look, kids, we know prohibition doesn't work, that it's cruel and costs so much we don't have anything left over with which to fight the social causes of addiction or treat the addicts, but, hey, it feels good, so we're going to keep right on doing it. To which the appropriate response is, of course, heh heh.

We don't have to quit cold turkey. We could start with marijuana, then ease up on cocaine and heroin possession, concentrating law enforcement on the big-time pushers. Take it slowly, see how it feels. One day at a time.

4
The War on Drugs Is Futile

Max Frankel

Max Frankel is a former executive editor for and a current contributing columnist for the New York Times.

The media have been too eager to endorse the war on drugs as a success. This war has been financially costly and has resulted in rampant crime and social decay in America's neighborhoods. The media should accurately portray the war on drugs as a futile effort so that legalization can be pursued.

I used to hate hearing about the "war" against drugs, and as executive editor tried to discourage that metaphor in the *New York Times*. But the politicians won the battle of the cliché even as they were losing the war. The "war" term appeared in this newspaper only 16 times in all of 1981, but 66 times in 1987 and 511 times in 1989, after President Bush promised at his inaugural, "Take my word for it, this scourge will stop." Well, it didn't, and we're down to about 100 mentions in each of the Clinton years, a mere twice a week. And now I'm sorry, for it's time the media began to cover the war on drugs as a war—the way they covered the last war that America lost.

The better newspapers are portraying the drug quagmire the way they once portrayed the quagmire in Vietnam. Dispatches from the front find cops risking life and limb to drag in users and dealers, but just as many stalk the streets the next night. The brass that's bragging about progress and calling for still more troops, weapons, prisons and money must be smoking something.

If the newspapers, magazines and TV networks would agree that there's a war on, maybe they would report a monthly "bag count"—the number of kilo-size packs of cocaine or heroin seized by Federal, state and local raiders in urban hideaways, remote marinas and canine stomachs. They could point out that the bag count, much like the Vietnam body count, is a meaningless index of progress in the war, no matter how impressive the seizures, the flow of bags in the underground drug channels continues relentlessly.

The press has been too generous with pictures of prosecutors and

Max Frankel, "O.K., Call It War," *The New York Times Magazine*, December 18, 1994.

politicians posing with the mounds of heroin and cocaine they've stumbled across somewhere. If more of the media would open drug-war bureaus in the inner cities, their bravest reporters would find that there's no shortage anytime, no increase at all in the street price of drugs, just constant pressure by a guerrilla army of street pushers supporting their own drug habit by enlarging the circle of customers. The reporters would document the cost and futility of the pursuit, the cynicism and corruption of the pursuers and the serene confidence of a wealthy enemy.

An unwinnable war

Gradually, maybe through C-Span "teach-ins" run by such radicals as former secretary of state George Shultz, Mayor Kurt L. Schmoke of Baltimore and William F. Buckley Jr., the commercial networks might learn that the war on drugs—meaning the prohibition of drugs—is not only being lost but is also unwinnable. The radicals have adopted the antiwar slogan of "legalization," but the TV anchors don't have to embrace that still-undefined remedy. They need only climb to the rooftops of Washington Heights in New York and cruise down along the Potomac Delta while reciting the terrifying findings of their research staffs: the direct, recognizable cost of this war is probably running in excess of $100 billion a year. There's not even a good estimate of the cost of the related crimes committed by drug peddlers and users, and of the measures taken to prevent such crimes, to compensate the victims and to punish some of the perpetrators. Hundreds of millions of dollars are being stashed in offshore sanctuaries and hundreds of millions more are available to import the stuff and to pave the way with bribes and untaxed wages.*

Of the 20 million American drug users, maybe 5 million are "seriously" addicted. A year's supply of heroin for all of them can be made from opium poppies grown on only 20 square miles of land—not quite the area of Manhattan. A year's supply of coke can be stashed in 13 truck trailers. So "eradicating" the supply abroad is impossible; "interdicting" drugs at the border is a joke.

The war on drugs—meaning the prohibition of drugs—is not only being lost but is also unwinnable.

About 40,000 Americans die each year of the direct and indirect effects of drugs; a large proportion of New York City's 2,000 annual homicides are attributable to drug trafficking. And drug offenders, whether or not they are violent criminals, clog the courts and prisons.

When finally one of the TV anchors senses that the country is ready to hear unvarnished truth, like Walter Cronkite's passionate declaration in 1968 that it was time to get out of Vietnam, she won't have to bother with statistics. Against a backdrop of gripping graphics, she could simply

* Most of the statistics in this viewpoint are taken from *The Making of a Drug-Free America* by Mathea Falco and "A Wiser Course: Ending Drug Prohibition, a Report of the Special Committee on Drugs and the Law of the Association of the Bar of the City of New York."

list the war's consequences:

- Urban blight, fear and destruction.
- Neighborhood turf wars and shootouts.
- Family ruin, school failure and wreckage.
- Lost productivity in the economy.
- Crack babies, kids dealing drugs, addicts felled by AIDS.
- Cops corrupted. Courts and prisons overwhelmed.
- Murder and mayhem clear to the top in Mexico, Colombia and other countries that cannot resist supplying the rich American market. And in America, contempt for government—and despair.

If the prohibition of drugs is a lost cause then "legalization"—in some form—is inevitable. But the word "legalization" has been demonized, like "negotiation" before Henry Kissinger sat down with the Vietcong in Paris. In 1993, Surgeon General Joycelyn Elders was pilloried—and disowned by her President—for recommending "some studies" of how drugs might be legalized and regulated. Most Americans still think legalization would constitute "surrender" to immorality. Some call it "genocide" because they imagine ghetto children lining up at the corner drugstore for their daily fix.

If the prohibition of drugs is a lost cause then "legalization"—in some form—is inevitable.

Not until we in the media do a better job of reporting the horrendous costs of this unwinnable war will the public consider alternative policies. By definition, legalizing drugs would put the big dealers and their gun-toting distributors out of business. It would also keep most users from having to steal to support the habit. That alone would liberate a great deal of money and energy for reclaiming wrecked lives and neighborhoods.

Like the Surgeon General, I don't pretend to know how a legal drug trade might be managed. Maybe drugs should be sold inexpensively to adults through Government outlets, like the ABC liquor stores that many states opened after Prohibition. Maybe drugs should be given away at neighborhood dispensaries that also offer treatment to cure addiction. Maybe dozens of experiments are in order.

By all means, let's call it "war." Then deal with defeat.

5

Legalizing Drugs Would Benefit the United States

Steven B. Duke and Albert C. Gross

Steven B. Duke is a professor at Yale University Law School in New Haven, Connecticut. Albert C. Gross is a lawyer in San Diego, California.

Drug legalization would benefit the United States in numerous ways. Among other benefits, it would save federal, state, and local governments billions of dollars a year; it would lead to reduced crime and safer neighborhoods; and it would result in the enhancement of public health. Because these benefits far outweigh the potential risks, drugs should be legalized.

"How can you conserve the basic values, how can you conserve the fabric of your life if you do not have the courage to change when what you're doing is tearing the heart out of your country?"

Presidential candidate Bill Clinton, in a speech to the National Urban League, San Diego, July 27, 1992[1]

Drug prohibition has not worked in the past, does not work now and will not work in the future. Recognition of that truth eventually will force drug-policy makers to legalize or at least de facto decriminalize the drugs now prohibited. What are the benefits and costs of the legalization option?

Benefits

Legalization will lead to at least eight beneficial outcomes:

Benefit number one: a saving of $200 billion or more per year The federal, state and local governments spend about $100 billion a year on law-enforcement and criminal-justice programs. About $35 billion of that is directly related to drug-law enforcement. Probably another $15 billion is related to crimes committed to obtain drug money or is otherwise systemically related to drug commerce. Hence, about $50 billion per year spent on law enforcement could be saved if drugs were legalized.

As Gore Vidal put it, "fighting drugs is nearly as big a business as pushing them."[2] Drug legalization threatens the jobs and career trajectories of police officers and politician-drug warriors. Defense attorneys and prosecutors, who make their living on drug cases, will also lose from drug legalization. Drug Enforcement Administration (DEA) officer Michael Levine exaggerated when he told CBS News: "The whole drug war is a political grab bag, in that everybody has got their arm in looking for that political jackpot that will either win them an election, win them a lucrative position as a consultant or you name it,"[3] but serious de-escalation of the drug war—to say nothing of legalization—does threaten tens of thousands of careers that the taxpayers would no longer need to support. That is a major impediment to legalization. Nonetheless, many law-enforcement officers are well ahead of politicians in recognizing the futility and economic wastefulness of the drug war. As Robert Stutman, previously a high official of the DEA, says, "Those of us who carry a badge learned a long time ago we're not going to solve the problem, and yet an awful lot of policy makers continue to depend on us, and we keep telling them we can't do it."[4]

Ralph Salerno, a famous organized-crime expert and long-time drug warrior himself, goes further. He says that the drug war not only "will never work" but that police on the front line, risking their lives and their physical, psychological and moral health, "are being lied to, just as I was lied to 20 years ago."[5] Among the lies:

> [P]olice officers and all other Americans are being told by our political leaders that if the coca crop in Peru and Bolivia can be curtailed it will be all over, ignoring the botanical fact that coca can be grown in many parts of the world. We are told that if the chemicals can be cut off from the purification plants in Colombia it will all be over. The chemicals are derivatives of the oil industry and there are wells in many parts of the world. We are told that if we can incarcerate the Medellin and Cali cartels it will all be over, and that is another lie. The Latin American *narcotraficantes* will be replaced by others as easily as were the American mafiosi.[6]

The waste of the public fisc on law enforcement pales in comparison to the costs of the drug war borne by individual citizens. Estimates of the yearly earnings of the illicit-drug business range as high as $100 billion. Sixty billion dollars may be a conservative estimate. Thus, if the principal recreational drugs were legal, drug consumers might save $60 to $100 billion each year.

Although nonusers may have difficulty sympathizing with a program that would make drug use more economical, in fact nonusers have a personal financial stake in drastic reductions in drug prices. Nonusers provide much of the money spent on drugs when they are innocent victims of crime. If $10 billion of the money spent to buy drugs comes from stolen tangible property—a rough estimate—property owners may lose $50 billion worth of property to provide the thieves with $10 billion in cash or equivalents with which to buy drugs (stolen property is sold at steep discounts). Nonusers also indirectly bear much of the cost of high drug prices when they pay high premiums for theft insurance, when they purchase security systems, when they pay high taxes for police protection and when they pay a premium to live in gated communities or suburbs. Inner-city landlords pay when their tenants move out to escape the hellishness of their surroundings.

Those users who do not perpetrate property crimes must spend their legitimate earnings on drugs. This often deprives their families of the money needed to survive. The non-drug-using public ends up paying for much of that distress, too. Welfare and public-health budgets also bear heavy burdens. Much of the $60 billion or more collected by drug traffickers from customers comes indirectly from the pockets of nonusers.

Adding the money squandered on the ineffective drug-suppression activities of state and federal governments to the money we all lose as a result of the unnaturally high price of drugs, the total probably would come to well over $150 billion per year, perhaps twice that. Drug legalization could save us most of that cost.

Drug legalization could produce an increase in property values in the cities that would make all other savings minuscule in comparison.

Moreover, drug prohibition is a major contributor to the destruction of our inner cities. Drug legalization could produce an increase in property values in the cities that would make all other savings minuscule in comparison. In city after city over the past several decades, hundreds of millions of dollars have been spent to "revitalize" or "renew" the inner city. Much of that money and most of the renewal projects only decelerated the decline that continued, apparently inexorably. Eliminating drug prohibition and the crime and insecurity it causes would do more to make the cities livable than everything spent on urban renewal in the past half century. The resulting increases in property values could number in the trillions of dollars.

Legalization will not alone solve the problem of inner-city decay and disintegration. It could even temporarily exacerbate the problem in some areas, where many of the residents survive on the drug trade: they sell drugs not only to other inner-city residents but, directly and indirectly, to white upper-class suburbanites.[7] While it saps resources from virtually every user sector, the drug trade also produces an important flow of money from the suburbs to sections of the inner city. Government and private agencies will have to replace some of that urban income in the form of jobs, training programs, public assistance and other investments in human capital. Even if the menace of drug-related crime is eliminated, the residents of the inner city must still have jobs, housing and quality schools in order for the cities to prosper. What legalization promises is a climate in which such basic elements for survival—and prosperity—are possible.

Benefit number two: reduced crime and safer neighborhoods The full costs of drug-prohibition crimes are measured in lives lost, neighborhoods destroyed, families shattered and the psychological penalties of living in a police state required to "protect" a society under siege. In neighborhoods both rich and poor, the specter of crime is omnipresent. In America's most disadvantaged neighborhoods, open-air drug markets and gang violence related to drug-turf battles make life miserable. Possibly as much as half of our violent and property crimes—certainly a very large portion—

would be eliminated by legalization.

The present prohibitionist policy has created a distorted and perverse economy in our inner cities. For the youngster growing up there, the models of upward mobility are not people who go to school to learn professions and trades, but drug peddlers who flash expensive jewelry and clothing. An enormous amount of human capital is being wasted. In the most obscene cases, children not yet in their teens are recruited as gofers and even assassins for drug gangs because they work cheaply and their juvenile status makes them immune to the full force of the law. An end to prohibition would remove both the model of the criminal entrepreneur and many of the incentives for infantile criminality. A reallocation of resources from drug interdiction to education and economic development of the inner city could create role models consistent with the high value our country places on the work ethic.

When the illicit drug business leaves the cities, our homes, streets and schools will become far safer. It may even become possible to educate children in urban public schools.

Benefit number three: elimination of drug-related corruption and waste Our drug laws are a major source of the corruption of public officials and law-enforcement officers. Respect for law is impossible when corruption is ubiquitous. Legalization would make a great source of official temptation disappear overnight.

Even if all public officials and law-enforcement officers were scrupulously honest, the war on drugs still would be extremely wasteful. Seizure of the assets of drug suspects is an example of the sort of drug-war inefficiency that is draining the national economy. One would think that the authority to take property without any due process would make drug-enforcement largely self-sustaining, if not actually profitable. However, this is not the case. The government's cash and noncash seizures in 1991 amounted to just over one billion dollars, or only 8.5 percent of the $12.5 billion the federal government spent on drug programs that year.[8]

What legalization promises is a climate in which . . . basic elements for survival—and prosperity—are possible.

Cash comprises only a fraction of the total appraised value of the assets seized. In 1991, approximately 64 percent of the dollar value of forfeitures was attributable to *non*cash assets—real estate, airplanes, motor vehicles, boats, negotiable instruments, jewelry.[9] When disposed of, these assets return a tiny fraction of their appraised value. General Accounting Office (GAO) investigators told Congress that the United States Customs actually lost money on over two thirds of the noncash items it seized between June 1987 and June 1989.[10]

How are such losses possible?

Customs had to remit $302 million worth of noncash, drug-war booty to the people from whom it was unjustly, illegally or improperly seized, and incurred storage and handling costs of $7.7 million in the process. Because so much of that property was seized illegally or taken from completely innocent bystanders, Customs was only able to charge remittees for $4.5 million of the handling costs, thereby realizing a net loss of $3.2 million on the returned property. Another $37.6 million worth of illegitimate seizures was "canceled" before Customs actually took possession, resulting in a loss of another $100,000 in handling costs.

Much of the property seized by Customs was worthless junk that was destroyed rather than sold, although its official appraised value came to $29 million. For instance, many of the automobiles seized by the Customs Service are in fact old clunkers that seizure-wary drug couriers tend to drive rather than the flashy cars we see in movies and on television.[11]

Customs keeps some of the property it seizes, and it gives some of that property to state and local law-enforcement agencies. Customs and the agencies also directly use the boats, vehicles and other equipment they retain. Accordingly, during the period covered by the GAO report, Customs retained (or gave to other police agencies) property that had an appraised value of $27.8 million. From the administrative costs and from an estimated rate of return on other assets that have been sold, the GAO calculates that the federal and state governments' net gain on those $27.8 million worth of property was only $7.2 million.

When the illicit drug business leaves the cities, our homes, streets and schools will become far safer.

During the two years covered by the GAO report, Customs managed to auction off less than 10 percent of the property it seized. But even then the financial waste was catastrophic. Contractors for the Customs Service sold $42.8 million worth of real estate, automobiles, boats, airplanes, jewelry, and appliances, but the taxpayer netted only $7.4 million or 17.2 percent of the property's appraised value. (One of the worst horror stories told to Congress involved a $170,000 boat that was sold for $13,500.[12]) Marketing and advertising costs—largely paid to government contractors—also contributed greatly to the government's losses on the Customs sales. And the government's warehousing costs are outrageous; the Customs Service has paid as much as $360 per month, for as long as a year, to store $1,000 drug boats.[13] The GAO reported that the U.S. Customs Service *lost* an average of $204 on each automobile seized, in the first three quarters of 1989.[14]

The final box score, according to GAO: "Property appraised at $438.9 million provided a return of 2 cents per dollar."[15] Only the government could perform so disastrously on a retail business for which all the merchandise is stolen from suppliers.

Legalization would put a stop to all this nonsense because it would terminate the property forfeitures.

Benefit number four: room in jails and prisons for real criminals About one third of the prisoners now stuffed into our penal institutions would not be there if it were no longer a crime to possess or traffic in the presently illicit drugs. An additional proportion of the other convicts—possibly another quarter—are in prison for property crimes committed to support drug habits. Still others are there for crimes of violence related to the drug business. If the drug-prohibition burden that has been superimposed on our penal system were removed, then the institutions would be available to punish the perpetrators of the sorts of crimes that truly threaten our security and freedom such as rape, murder, robbery and burglary.[16]

If drugs are legalized, the dangers to physical health from using heroin, cocaine, marijuana or other previously illegal drugs would be greatly *reduced.*

Benefit number five: enhanced public health Drug prohibition deprives us of the medicinal use of marijuana, heroin and other drugs. Drug prohibition makes the inevitable use of psychotropic drugs more dangerous. Most overdoses and drug poisonings are attributable to the operation of the illicit market, not to the inherent qualities of drugs. Further, needle sharing by intravenous drug users now does as much or more to spread HIV and hepatitis infections as do unsafe sexual practices. And America's drug puritanism has widely blocked the implementation of clean-needle programs that clearly reduce the spread of AIDS and other deadly diseases.[17] Drug prohibition has also kept drug users from seeking treatment for many other medical conditions, many of which are communicable. The illegal status of drugs even makes it more difficult for drug abusers to seek treatment for drug addiction, the very condition that often inspires them to commit the crimes of drug possession and trafficking.

If drugs are legalized, the dangers to physical health from using heroin, cocaine, marijuana or other previously illegal drugs would be *greatly* reduced. Even if such drug use were to increase by a factor of two or three, the deaths and diseases caused by such drug use would still be lower than they are now. Also, since the economic factors pushing producers, traffickers and users toward more concentrated, more deadly and more addictive drugs would be eliminated by legalization, one can expect many users to confine their drug consumption to highly diluted forms, just as consumers of alcohol more often drank beer before and after alcohol prohibition than they did during Prohibition. This alone will greatly reduce the health risks and the addictive potential of drug use under a legalized system. If drug purities were standardized and clearly and accurately labeled, the likelihood of a person accidentally overdosing would be much less than it is under the present regime.

Legalizing heroin, cocaine and marijuana would probably produce a net reduction in the use of tobacco and alcohol, saving thousands of lives every year, perhaps tens of thousands. This reduction would come from two sources. First, as prohibitionists commonly argue, legalizing the illegal drugs would convey a message that the legal and illegal drugs are in the same socio-cultural-medical family. Some of the billions that the government has spent trying to convince us that illegal drugs are immoral, suicidal, treasonous, dumb and so forth will be symbolically transferred to legal drugs, causing some potential drinkers or smokers to think long and hard before using or abusing those drugs as well. Second, many of the illegal drugs are substitutes for alcohol, and vice versa. Studies demonstrate that when access to alcohol is restricted—as when the drinking age was raised from eighteen to twenty-one—there is a substantial corresponding increase in the consumption of marijuana, not otherwise explainable.[18] This strongly suggests that increased availability of marijuana would reduce alcohol consumption.

Similarly, when heroin addicts are deprived of heroin, they become alcohol abusers.[19] Making heroin more available would probably decrease the number of alcohol abusers. If legalization produces an increase in the consumption of illegal drugs, some of the increase may represent a transfer from alcohol or even tobacco. To the extent the switch is into marijuana, that would be a major plus, as far as health is concerned, and that could even be true of a switch from alcohol or tobacco to cocaine or heroin, hard as that may be for some to accept.[20] But even if no such transfers from legal to previously illegal drugs occurred, the first factor mentioned above might produce a reduction in smoking and drinking.

Benefit number six: restored civil liberties and respect for law Americans are less free than they were before drug prohibition began in 1914. Each year, as some supposed "loophole" used by drug dealers is closed, we all lose important civil liberties. Many Americans are persuaded by the claims of drug police and prosecutors that we must sacrifice constitutional safeguards in order to keep drug felons from escaping on "technicalities." However, the "technicalities" are the substance of our liberty, which took a revolution to establish. If drugs were legalized, there would be much less reason for police and prosecutors to seek, and for courts and legislatures to provide, easier standards for imposing criminal punishment, forfeitures and other deprivations of fundamental freedom.

Ridding our courts of the glut of drug and drug-related criminal cases will permit them to attend to civil matters, largely neglected in our escalated drug war. People who are injured in automobile or other accidents or are the victims of malpractice, fraud, rape or battery won't have to wait five to ten years for a court decision. Defendants who are accused of crime may once again entertain an expectation of getting a fair trial. Those who are convicted can even hope to obtain a fair and honest review of their convictions by courts of appeal.

Benefit number seven: drug prosecutions will no longer destroy the lives of otherwise productive citizens Most users of presently illegal drugs, like most users of tobacco and alcohol, are productive, generally law-abiding people. But making their drug consumption a serious crime makes it harder for them to be so, and makes it impossible for some to be so—those who are socially and economically marginal to begin with. Legalizing drugs would greatly increase the capacity of the 26 million users of presently illicit drugs to be productive citizens.

About 500,000 of our jail and prison inmates are there for illegal-drug or drug-related offenses. Possibly as many as 300,000 would not be there if drug prohibition were repealed because they would not be criminals under legalization. They would be available to their spouses and children, helping to raise families left parentless by imprisonment. Many of these people would be useful members of society rather than embittered criminals wracked with rage over their unjust punishment. No one who gets a prison term of any duration for using drugs and no one who gets a twenty-year prison term, or even a five-year term, for selling drugs to a willing buyer is likely to be persuaded that his punishment was deserved. Hundreds of thousands of Americans who might otherwise be integrated into the mainstream of society have that possibility virtually eliminated by a combination of embitterment and societal stigma, rendering their acceptance of and by the mainstream unlikely. This appalling waste of human lives, which far exceeds any plausible cost of illegal-drug use, would be eliminated by legalization.

Benefit number eight: users will bear most of the costs When reformers were lobbying for drug prohibition early in the twentieth century, they justified their proposal on the ground that it would protect drug users from the damage caused by their own folly or depravity. The prohibition laws obviously do not prevent moderately determined drug buyers from harming themselves with drugs, and in the waning years of the twentieth century, compassion for the less fortunate has become an increasingly difficult commodity to sell to the American public anyway. Hence, the major justification that prohibitionists now offer for continuing prohibition is that it protects *non*users from harm. The harm that the prohibitionists wish to spare us takes two forms: victimization by crime and financial loss. Yet, we already have described how prohibition *causes* both categories of harm, rather than protecting us from them.

One of the most ironic consequences of prohibition is that it virtually guarantees that innocent victims will pay the financial cost of the harm that prohibition unsuccessfully seeks to prevent. This is because no taxes are collected on drug commerce, and law enforcement does everything it can to pauperize drug users, so they are not financially responsible for any of the damage they cause.

Scholars who study the relationship of law and economics have coined the term "cost externalization" to describe phenomena akin to this consequence of prohibition.[21] When the costs of a commodity are internalized, those who profit from producing the commodity are required to pay the costs for the damage that the commodity causes. Thus, when manufacturers are forced to pay for injuries caused by defective products, that particular cost of the enterprise has been internalized. To the extent that motorists, automobile manufacturers and oil companies pay less than the full costs of road construction, use of land for parking, automobile accidents and the damage caused by air pollution, they have externalized the costs of the activity from which they benefit.

As matters stand under drug prohibition, drug users and sellers can externalize almost all the harm costs of their activity. Prohibitionist propaganda over the past few years has suggested that asset forfeitures compensate the government for drug-enforcement costs. However, we saw earlier that the government actually loses money on many seizures, and makes little on most, so sellers and users even externalize the costs of enforcing prohibition. The general taxpayer picks up most of the tab. No tax money comes in from drug commerce to pay for the costs of drug education and treatment of drug abusers. Drug sellers and buyers pay no direct tax to offset the medicaid and welfare costs of supporting impoverished addicts. Drug dealers don't even pay income taxes on their profits.

Harvard Medical School professor Lester Grinspoon has proposed that America institute "harm taxes" to internalize some of the costs for the damage done by drugs.[22] His proposal is consistent with recent efforts to increase taxes on legal drugs, in order to internalize some of the harm caused by alcohol and tobacco. For instance, in 1988, California voters approved Proposition 99,[23] a referendum that imposed a quarter-per-pack tax increase on cigarettes and dedicated the revenue to antismoking public education and other measures to alleviate tobacco harm. Dr. Grinspoon's measure would work with regard to the now-contraband drugs only if they were legalized. Indeed, one of the principal benefits to be realized from drug legalization would be the ability to tax drugs so their harm costs might be partly internalized.

Risks (costs) of legalization

Increased consumption of presently illegal drugs Drug consumption could soar under legalization. Yet that prospect is extremely unlikely. Legalizing drugs would not be a reckless experiment.

During most of its history, this country had no drug prohibition, and drug abuse was never worse than it is now. There are few countries in the history of the world that ever had a majority of their populations hooked on any drug other than tobacco, and when they did, it was alcohol. Drugs are still at least de facto legal on much of the globe, as they have been throughout most of human history; yet if there is or ever has been a country that has 10 percent of its population abusing cocaine or heroin, we have not heard of it. Although there are legal prohibitions against drug trafficking in our neighbor to the south, Mexico, there is no serious enforcement against local distribution or consumption. Mexico is a major source of marijuana and heroin, and a major transshipment point for cocaine. The country is awash in inexpensive drugs. Yet our own State Department says that Mexico "does not have a serious drug problem."[24] Regular, heavy use of strong psychoactive do-it-yourself drugs is either an effort to treat mental illness or an effort to escape pain and despair, or both. The notion that any drug, if freely available, will enslave an entire population has no basis in fact or theory. It is prohibitionist fantasy.

Recent Netherlands experience suggests that abandoning suppression efforts need not even produce new users. That country de facto decriminalized marijuana. While possession and use of marijuana technically is still a crime in Holland, one can purchase hashish and marijuana there with impunity. Some Amsterdam cafés blatantly feature various forms of cannabis on their menus, and municipal recreational facilities for teenagers can sell as much as thirty grams to their young patrons without being prosecuted.[25] According to a 1989 report by the United States Embassy in the Hague[26] and a 1985 report by the Dutch government,[27] marijuana consumption in the Netherlands has *decreased* substantially since the decriminalization.

At various times, eleven American states more or less decriminalized possession and use of marijuana.[28] Yet marijuana consumption has declined at approximately the same rate in the states that decriminalized it as consumption has declined elsewhere in the United States.[29]

Marijuana has decreased in the Netherlands and in states that decriminalized for the same reasons its use has declined in places that have retained prohibition. People stopped using marijuana, or use it to a lesser extent, because "pot smoking" is simply less fashionable than it once was, and because of heightened health consciousness. What these experiences demonstrate is that extralegal, psychosocial forces account for changes in patterns of drug consumption far more than do prohibition efforts; that official suppression—or lack thereof—is a relatively uninfluential factor in drug-use trends and patterns. This is corroborated by a random telephone survey of 1,401 American adults conducted in 1990. Of those Americans polled, fewer than 1 in 100 who had not tried cocaine would do so if it were legal.[30]

Since eliminating (or greatly shrinking) the black market in drugs is the main object of legalization, drug prices under a system of legalization, even though taxed, must be kept much lower than they are now. When most commodities become cheaper, more people use them and those who used them before use more of them. That is true to some extent when the commodity is a pleasure drug. We observed that with the invention of crack in the mid-1980s, when the cost of a cocaine high was drastically reduced, bringing in hordes of new users. In July 1992, the *New York Times* reported that due in part to the recent abundance of heroin and cocaine (despite decades of drug war aimed at preventing it), drug dealers had cut the price of a $10 or "dime" bag of heroin to $5 and, in some parts of the city, reduced the price of a dose of crack to an all-time low of 75 cents.[31] New York authorities believe that the reduced prices also accompanied increases in the numbers of both new users and abusers of cocaine. Heroin use also increased as prices declined, because users could afford to snort heroin rather than inject it and thus avoided the risk of AIDS and several other diseases related to intravenous drug use. Several studies show that the price of cigarettes—our most addictive drug—has a measurable impact upon consumption, especially long term: the higher the price, other things being equal, the less tobacco is smoked.[32] Reducing the amount of money it takes to buy a dose of a drug is not the only cost reduction to the user contemplated by legalization. The user under legalization will no longer be a felon for using drugs and will no longer feel pressured to commit crimes in order to pay for the drugs used. Thus, in a broad sense, the "price" of drug use under legalization will be vastly reduced. There is undoubtedly a causal relationship between drug usage and drug prices, especially over the short term.

Legalizing drugs would greatly increase the capacity of the 26 million users of presently illicit drugs to be productive citizens.

Legalizing the use of a drug that was previously criminal is also likely to have some influence in the direction of increasing consumption beyond its effects on the availability of drugs. Laws still have some impact upon the behavior of some citizens, even if such laws are widely disregarded by large segments of society. While legalizing drugs is not a statement that using drugs is desirable—the government regularly propagandizes against many activities that are legal, including smoking, dropping out of school, unsafe sex and so forth—legalization can be interpreted by some potential drug users as withdrawing condemnation, even as morally equating the use of newly legalized drugs with those already legal, such as tobacco and alcohol. This too can have a contributing influence on the consumption of previously illegal drugs (and, as noted earlier, a negative influence on consumption of previously legal drugs).

There is, therefore, a substantial likelihood that, *all other things remaining equal*, legalization will be accompanied by an increase in the consumption of newly legalized drugs. But there is also little reason, and no support in what followed the repeal of alcohol prohibition, to suggest that legalizing the illegal drugs would produce a huge increase in the numbers of users of pleasure drugs or, more important, the numbers of *abusers* of such drugs. One who neither smokes tobacco nor drinks alcohol is extremely unlikely to become a user of any of the other pleasure drugs (caffeine aside). While there are surely some teetotalers or occasional light drinkers who would become addicted to heroin or cocaine under a system of legalization, their numbers are almost certainly small. The major reasons why people desist from smoking and drinking—health, social stigma, morality, aesthetics—are also applicable to other pleasure drugs.

The potential new users of legalized drugs are therefore people who are now deterred by the price of these drugs or by the criminality of their use, but who nonetheless drink or smoke cigarettes.* To the extent that such persons were to substitute newly legalized pleasure drugs for tobacco or alcohol, they would be better off from a bodily health standpoint, and so would those who come into contact with them. Cocaine or heroin users do not pollute the air and rarely beat up their spouses or children while intoxicated on those drugs.

Most of the people who would abuse cocaine or heroin if it were legalized, but who do not now abuse these drugs, are already abusing alcohol, killing themselves and others by the tens of thousands every year. They would be less likely to kill themselves with drugs if they used less alcohol, even if they used more cocaine or heroin, and would be much less likely to kill the rest of us.[33]

It seems clear that increased consumption of marijuana or heroin, all other conditions remaining the same, will result in a reduction in the consumption of alcohol. The psychoactive effects of such drugs are sufficiently similar to alcohol, among a large number of users, that they are to a substantial extent substitutes. What is less clear is whether such a relationship exists between cocaine and alcohol. A great many cocaine users also consume alcohol while taking cocaine; the two drugs are apparently complementary, one being a depressant and the other a stimulant. Alcohol, which is cheap, may augment the effects of cocaine, which is expensive. Alcohol thus seems to play a role similar to that of Hamburger Helper. It is not as good as the real thing, but it helps to stretch out the

* Many nonusers—even though they smoke or drink—may also be deterred by the health risk of drug use, which would be greatly reduced under any rational system of legalization. Offsetting that factor, however, is that drugs would contain labels warning of the dangers of using the particular drug. Thus, drugs would be safer under legalization but their residual dangers would be better known and effectively advertised.

real thing with tolerable diluting effects. We think it is likely, however, that increased use of cocaine will not be accompanied by an increased use of alcohol but rather a reduction. If cocaine is inexpensive, as it would be under legalization, there would be little incentive to use alcohol as a stretcher or helper of cocaine. More important, perhaps, combining either heroin and cocaine with alcohol is dangerous. Most deaths from "overdoses" of cocaine and heroin may in reality be overdoses of alcohol (or barbiturates) *and* cocaine or heroin (or both).[34] Users would be better informed about the risks of drug synergy under legalization. The kick or sensation that alcohol adds to cocaine would not be worth the risks in a legalized system, since cocaine itself would be approximately the same price per intoxicating dose as alcohol.

The very substantial reductions in numbers of alcohol and tobacco users over the past few decades demonstrates that people are capable of avoiding drugs that they know are bad for them, even if the government says they are legal and they are widely advertised as the key to success and happiness. As federal judge Robert W. Sweet observed in a 1989 speech urging drug legalization, "If our society can learn to stop using butter, it should be able to cut down on cocaine."[35]

Whether Americans choose to avoid recreational drugs in the first place or to quit using or abusing them is linked to the quality of their lives and their perceived prospects for a rewarding life without drug use or abuse. This is clearly demonstrated by recent data about illegal-drug use. Illegal-drug use has been reduced drastically in the past few years among white middle and upper classes—but hardly or not at all among ethnic minorities, who largely inhabit our inner cities. Many of those users see nothing but a bleak future before them. They have little to lose by drug abuse, and they proceed to lose it.

In sum, the drug market is already saturated with a combination of legal and illegal drugs. Virtually everyone who now wants to get high already does so. Legalization may significantly alter market shares among the now legal and illegal drugs, but it is unlikely to create a strong surge in *new* demand for psychoactive drugs. As Michael S. Gazzaniga, professor of neuroscience at Dartmouth Medical School, puts it, "There is a base rate of drug abuse, and it is [presently] achieved one way or another."[36]

Even if heroin, cocaine and marijuana legalization increased substantially the number of users of such drugs and even their total drug consumption, the number of abusers of such drugs could still be diminished by legalization. The drugs used would probably be less potent than those now available and therefore less addictive and less damaging. Users of legal drugs also have many advantages over users of illegal drugs that help them to resist frequent, heavy use. They need not be criminals or outcasts to use the drugs. They are less likely to acquire serious or incapacitating illnesses from drug use. They need not steal to buy their drugs; they can work at a regular, legitimate job. Legal-drug use, therefore, is far more compatible with the personal ties, extrinsic resources and general well-being that support efforts to resist drug abuse.

Other risks There are no other major risks of legalization apart from increased consumption of drugs. All other risks are subsidiaries. Some of the derivative risks deserve mention, however. If legalization were to produce major long-run increases in the numbers of psychoactive-drug abusers—an assumption we have difficulty making for reasons already set forth—a number of concrete adverse consequences might follow. Many heroin and cocaine abusers, like alcoholics, have difficulty holding jobs or handling other significant responsibilities. Some of them—like many alcoholics—seem all but immune to treatment or other therapeutic interventions. Such persons have more than their share of health problems, and could put an additional strain on our health care systems. If legalization were to produce hundreds of thousands of new addicts who were incapable of functioning in the society, along with the mentally ill, alcohol and other drug-abusing derelicts who already inhabit our cities, this would indeed be a major cost of legalization. But for reasons already discussed, neither common sense nor experience supports the likelihood of such a scenario.

Legalizing drugs would not be a reckless experiment.

Some say that legalization would be the equivalent of genocide on inner-city black communities. But to believe that members of a particular race of Americans are incapable of making their own decisions about what they want to put into their bodies is reminiscent of the attitudes that underlay a system of slavery. Urban blacks are disproportionately users and abusers of both crack and heroin. But it does not follow that there is something in their genes or even in black culture that preordains such drug usage. People—regardless of their race—abuse drugs for two reasons: (1) they got hooked accidentally and haven't yet mustered the motivation and external assistance to quit, and/or (2) such abuse provides temporary escape from a painful existence. Prohibition can't change either of those circumstances, but a caring society, using funds freed by legalization, can change them both. Drug abuse can produce dreadful disabilities, with resultant neglect of children, jobs, health and other responsibilities, but drugs are not viruses or even bacteria: they are substances that people choose to take into their bodies. The first step in reducing drug abuse is to make sure that those who make the decisions to take drugs are aware of the risks of doing so. (This was not the case with crack; the epidemic was well underway before the addictive qualities of crack were widely known.) The second step is to provide a society in which the risks of using the drugs are unacceptable because life has more to offer than a chemical high. The notion that inner-city blacks lack the capacity to resist their own self-destruction is preposterous, yet it is just beneath the surface in prohibitionist polemics linking legalization and genocide. In addition to their painful lives, a major reason why inner-city blacks are heavy users of cocaine and heroin is that they are inundated by these drugs and their users. Most retail drug markets in the nation are located on the streets of the inner cities, the same streets in which children are growing up and trying to play. The children are often recruited as dealers before they become users. These markets would disappear under legalization.

Another subsidiary risk is that, if use of newly legalized drugs became far more widespread than at present, there would be greatly enlarged safety risks to nonusers. Automobiles, trucks, airplanes, factory machinery would be operated by people whose capacities were significantly impaired by drugs. But as we have noted, the major impairments are produced by alcohol, not the other drugs. If legalization diverts users from alcohol, we may even have safer highways and airways as a result. But it is, in any event, possible to prohibit driving and piloting by drug-impaired persons in a state of legalization. In fact, it would be less difficult under legalization because impaired operators would have less reason than they now do—when mere use of the drugs is a serious crime—to hide their condition. Drug testing is now commonplace—far more so than we would like—but in a state of legalization, drug testing by employers and traffic police would be much less objectionable, since it would not expose the person tested to a charge of a serious felony. Moreover, modern technology is capable of producing portable devices to test cognitive, perceptual and motor capacities. Such tests are far more relevant to one's ability to operate machinery than a test to determine the presence, or even the quantity, of drugs in one's blood, breath or urine.

Legalizing drugs does not require that impaired driving also be made legal. Drivers who are seriously impaired, for whatever reasons, should not drive and should be punished if they do so.

It is sometimes said that legalization will produce more "crack babies" or other infants whose health is seriously damaged by their mothers' drug use during pregnancy.[37] But much—perhaps most—of the damage done to such babies comes from their mothers' neglect of nutrition and hygiene, combined with the fact that many of them have no prenatal medical care. Fear of criminal prosecution keeps many such mothers away from prenatal care when it is available. Moreover, most drug-treatment programs, believe it or not, refuse access to pregnant mothers![38] Such idiocy would stop under any rational system of legalization.

When all benefits are combined, the case for legalization becomes overwhelming.

Finally, what about our children? Is it possible that the high cost of illegal drugs is a significant deterrent to drug experimentation by America's teenagers? If this cost were drastically reduced, a substantial segment of such deterrables might experiment with newly legalized drugs and become hooked. What we have already said about adults applies here as well. Children who do not drink or smoke will not use cocaine or heroin, however cheap it is. Many of those who do drink or smoke, and are interested in expanding their use of drugs, already have tried marijuana and many have tried cocaine. The price of experimental quantities of illegal drugs is already well within the reach of most teenagers.

Moreover, as difficult as it may be for some to contemplate, even if legalization produced a substantial increase in juvenile experimentation with marijuana, heroin or cocaine, the juveniles themselves, and the rest of society, might still be better off. Tobacco and alcohol are especially harmful to children's bodies; a reduction in the use of those drugs by juveniles would be a great advance, even if achieved by some increase in the use of other drugs.

We would continue to criminalize the distribution of drugs, including tobacco and alcohol, to children. But since drug use among adults would be lawful, we could concentrate our law-enforcement resources on purveyors of drugs to children, and we could be far more successful in that endeavor, having narrowed our focus, than we are today. It is not true that anything a society permits adults to do cannot effectively be denied children, and that, as a result, adults who encourage children to engage in such "adult" activities cannot be condemned. Sex between adults and children is severely condemned in America, while sex between unmarried adults is not even a misdemeanor in most states. We would treat the distribution of drugs to children like statutory rape, and put people in prison for it. Under today's prohibition that rarely happens.

The balance of benefits and costs

We think almost any one of the eight benefits we have sketched above outweighs the risks of legalization—which are not great. When all benefits are combined, the case for legalization becomes overwhelming. If legalization is too large a leap, courageous governors and a courageous president could give us many of the benefits of legalization simply by de-escalating the war. Cut the drug-law-enforcement budgets by two thirds (as President Clinton cut the personnel of the "drug" czar's office), stop civil forfeitures, grant executive clemency to most of the nonviolent drug violators stuffing our prisons, and much of the evil of prohibition will disappear. When the benefits of de-escalation are experienced, the nation will then be ready for de jure reform.

The meekest among us must admit that the case for legalizing marijuana is overwhelming. Jimmy Carter was right when he proposed decriminalization during his presidency.[39] We would all be better off if he had succeeded. Marijuana poses some health risks, but far less than tobacco or alcohol, and it substitutes for and therefore competes with both alcohol and tobacco. Pending the legalization of marijuana, our nation's chief executives and law-enforcement officers should put a stop to all prosecution for marijuana possession or trafficking, and open the prison doors for all who are there solely for such offenses. Even an ardent prohibitionist ought to agree with this proposal. Everyone agrees that cocaine and heroin are worse drugs, by any standards, than marijuana. If marijuana is legalized, the drug warriors could then focus their resources on the war against "hard" drugs.

The case for legalization is strong; the case for de-escalating the drug war is overwhelming.

Notes

1. Gwen Ifill, "Clinton Resists Being Labeled Liberal," *New York Times*, 28 July 1992.
2. Gore Vidal, *Homage to Daniel Shays: Collected Essays, 1952–1972* (New York: Random House, 1972), 375.
3. Richard Schlesinger, "CBS Evening News with Dan Rather," 29 March 1990.
4. Ibid.

5. Ralph F. Salerno, "The Anger of a Retired Chief Detective," in Arnold S. Trebach and Kevin B. Zeese, eds., *Drug Prohibition and the Conscience of Nations* (Washington, D.C.: The Drug Policy Foundation, 1990), 208, 209.
6. Ibid.
7. Jose deCordoba, "Carriage Trade, Big City Drug Dealers Draw Lots of Business from Suburban Buyers," *Wall Street Journal*, 19 November 1992.
8. United States Bureau of Justice Statistics, "Fact Sheet: Drug Data Summary," in *Drugs & Crime Data Center & Clearinghouse* (Washington, D.C.: Department of Justice, Office of Justice Programs, Bureau of Justice Statistics, November 1991), 1.
9. Ibid.
10. Statement of Richard L. Fogel, Assistant Comptroller General for General Government Programs, "Profitability of Customs Forfeiture Program Can Be Enhanced," *United States General Accounting Office Testimony*, 10 October 1989, 5, 9. Also see Robert A. Rosenblatt, "Seized Property Costs U.S., Panel Told," *Los Angeles Times*, 11 October 1989.
11. Fogel, "Profitability of Customs Forfeiture Program," 15.
12. Ibid., 18.
13. Rosenblatt, "Seized Property Costs U.S."
14. Fogel, 14.
15. Ibid., 9.
16. See Herbert Packer, *The Limits of the Criminal Sanction* (Stanford: Stanford University Press, 1968).
17. See Tamara Lytle, "Feds Blast City's Needle Exchange," *New Haven Register*, 10 July 1992.
18. Peter Passell, "Economic Scene: Less Marijuana, More Alcohol?" *New York Times*, 17 June 1992; John DiNardo and Thomas Lemieux, "Alcohol, Marijuana, and American Youth: The Unintended Consequences of Government Regulation" (Working Draft for RAND's Drug Policy Research Center, March 1992).
19. Edward Brecher and the editors of *Consumer Reports, Licit and Illicit Drugs* (Boston: Little, Brown, and Company, 1972), 85–89; Mark Kleiman, *Against Excess: Drug Policy for Results* (New York: Basic Books, 1992), 260.
20. For more on drug switching, see James Ostrowski, "Thinking About Drug Legalization," in David Boaz, *The Crises in Drug Prohibition* (Washington, D.C.: Cato Institute, 1990), 45, 63–64.
21. See Guido Calabresi, "Views and Overviews," *University of Illinois Law Forum*, 1967, 606.
22. *The Harmfulness Tax: A Proposal for Regulation and Taxation of Drugs: Hearings on Legalization of Drugs Before the Select Committee on Narcotics Abuse and Control*, 100th Congress, 1st Session (1988) (statement of Lester Grinspoon, M.D.).
23. California Health & Safety Code §424.10 (Deering 1991). See also further implementing legislation at California Health & Safety Code §24164 (Deering 1991).

24. Bureau of International Narcotics Matters, *International Narcotics Control Strategy Report, March 1991* (Washington, D.C.: Department of State, 1991), 156.

25. Rone Tempest, "Bold Experiment: Drugs: Dutch Gain with a Tolerant Tack." *Los Angeles Times*, 22 September 1989.

26. Ibid.

27. "Policy on Drug Users," (Rijswijk, the Netherlands: Ministry of Welfare, Health, and Cultural Affairs, 1985).

28. In Alaska, a court decision, *Ravin v. State*, 537 P.2d 494 (1975), allowed possession for individual use. In 1991, after fifteen years of lobbying by federal government drug warriors, Alaska voters, by a narrow margin, recriminalized the use of marijuana.

29. Lloyd D. Johnston, Jerald G. Bachman, Patrick M. O'Malley, "Marijuana Decriminalization: The Impact on Youth 1975–1980" (Ann Arbor: Monitoring the Future, Occasional Paper 13, 1981). See also Mark Kleiman, *Marijuana: Costs of Abuse, Costs of Control* (New York: Greenwood Press, 1989), 176; Eric W. Single, "Impact of Marijuana Decriminalization: An Update," *Journal of Public Health Policy*, 10, no. 4 (Winter 1989).

30. Richard Dennis, "The American People Are Starting to Question the Drug War," in Arnold Trebach and Kevin Zeese, eds., *Drug Prohibition and the Conscience of Nations* (Washington, D.C.: Drug Policy Foundation, 1990), 217, 218.

31. Joseph Treaster, "Hospital Visits by Drug Users Rise Sharply," *New York Times*, 9 July 1992.

32. United States Surgeon General, *Reducing the Health Consequences of Smoking: 25 Years of Progress, A Report of the Surgeon General* (Rockville, MD: Department of Health and Human Services, 1989), 536–39.

33. Even thoughtful analysts who oppose legalization agree on this point. See John Kaplan, *The Hardest Drug: Heroin and Public Policy* (The University of Chicago Press, 1983); Mark Kleiman, *Against Excess: Drug Policy for Results* (New York: Basic Books, 1992), 260, 362.

34. See Brecher et al., *Licit and Illicit Drugs*, 111–14; Linda W. Wong and Bruce K. Alexander, "Cocaine Related Deaths. Who Are the Victims? What Is the Cause?" in Arnold Trebach and Kevin Zeese, eds., *Drug Policy 1989–1990: A Reformers Catalogue* (Washington, D.C.: The Drug Policy Foundation, 1989), 177.

35. Stephen Labaton, "Federal Judge Urges Legalization of Crack, Heroin, and Other Drugs," *New York Times*, 13 December 1989.

36. "Opium of the People: The Federal Drugstore," *National Review*, 5 February 1990, 34.

37. See A.M. Rosenthal, "On My Mind, Captive Neighborhood," *New York Times*, 10 July 1992.

38. Gina Kolata, "Bias Seen Against Pregnant Addicts," *New York Times*, 20 July 1990.

39. Jean Seligman with Lucy Howard, "Easing the Pot Laws," *Newsweek*, 28 March 1977, 76.

6

Legalizing Drugs Would Reduce Drug-Related Crime

Bill Killion

Bill Killion is serving a sixty-three-month prison sentence at the Federal Correctional Institution in Fort Worth, Texas, for a drug-related offense.

Those who use illegal drugs are undeterred by threats of prison and, if convicted and sentenced for drug trafficking or use, they will return to using and trafficking when they are released. Legalizing drugs would decrease drug-related crime and reduce the number of people in prison for drug offenses.

I am a 35-year-old white male from a white-collar family. I'm educated, well balanced and rational, healthy, and intelligent. I am also a "drug addict" who has been "abusing" so-called "hard drugs" such as morphine, heroin and cocaine for the last 18 years.

Presently, I am serving a 63-month prison sentence at the Federal Correctional Institution located in Fort Worth, Texas, the result of a drug manufacturing and trafficking conviction. I have 33 months remaining on my sentence. This is my fifth trip to prison because of my involvement with drugs.

At this point you may be asking, "Well, have you learned anything of value from your incarceration, and do you plan to abstain from drugs when you are released?" My answer to those questions are yes and no, respectively.

What I have learned is that the American people are largely misinformed in reference to drugs, crime, and the war on drugs. This is due in the most part from their being brainwashed and duped with hype and propaganda by government officials who have a vested interest in keeping drugs illegal. The government blames as many of society's problems as possible, particularly crime, on drugs and drug addicts in order to keep the voting public's opinion swayed against drugs so the government can continue to keep drugs illegal because the illegal drug trade and its consequences are big business for the big government.

Anyone who thinks otherwise had best wake up and take a real good

Bill Killion, "Drug-Related Crime: Who Is to Blame?" *Anarchy: A Journal of Desire Armed*, Fall 1992. Reprinted with permission of B. A. L. Press, PO Box 2647 Stuyvesant Station, New York, NY 10185.

look around. Do you really think that the government cares if some drug addict murders you out of desperation to get money to pay the high price for his drugs that the illegal status of drugs continues to inflate more with each passing day? Think about it. Your untimely death from so-called "drug-related violence" helps them greatly in many ways. For example, it:

1. Makes available inheritance tax for the government.
2. Opens a job slot for one of the previously unemployed.
3. Decreases the population.
4. Adds one more false "drugs create violent crime" statistic to their war on drugs hype.
5. Helps the government justify its hiring of more law enforcement workers.
6. Adds to the conservative U.S. Supreme Court's excuse for putting greater adverse restrictions on our constitutional rights, which they gladly do in furtherance of their conspiracy to implement a total police-state in our country.
7. Generates income for numerous individuals and businesses including your local ambulance service, hospital, funeral parlor, casket company, cemetery, florist, attorney, etc., and all their employees.

Any American of moderate intelligence should be able to see through all of this bureaucratic war on drugs B.S., and many do. But the majority of society does not see through it because we have been systematically conditioned from birth to believe that our government is some wise, all-knowing, omnipotent body who can do no wrong—a power whose judgment and action we should not question.

Drugs do not cause crime, the illegal *status of drugs causes all of the so-called "drug-related crime."*

Concerning my future abstinence from drugs upon being released from prison—not a chance. I have been drug-free during these first two years of my incarceration and will remain drug-free until released, but only because using drugs in prison is too much of a hassle due to being in close quarters with an 85% population of eager stool pigeons. However, I look forward to being able to exercise my personal choice to use drugs again after being released, regardless of the current penalty. Over 99% of the drug-related prisoners feel the way I do.

When I use drugs, I don't have to worry about smelling like regurgitated alcohol, driving recklessly and killing an innocent driver, passenger or pedestrian, or losing my temper and behaving like an ass, and I don't have to wake up in the afternoon from a night out, wondering what all kinds of horribly embarrassing antics or quasi-criminal acts I may have carried out. Can any of you alcoholic beverage fans out there say the same? Not if you're honest.

Drugs and crime

Drugs do not cause crime, the *illegal* status of drugs causes all of the so-called "drug-related crime." Prior to the enactment of the Harrison Act in the early part of this century, which was the first real attempt to control drugs, we didn't have drug-turf wars or drive-by shootings. Nor did we have people committing thefts, burglaries, robberies and murders in order to obtain drugs, or money for drugs. It is an obvious and proven fact that so-called "drug-related crime" decreases and increases in direct proportion to the illicit drug price index, which in turn decreases or increases in direct proportion to the current severity of punishment being meted out to drug traffickers by the government for controlled substance violations.

If you want more "drug crime" in terms of both quantity and severity, then by all means keep pushing for tougher drug laws, and don't let the fact that your taxes will have to be continually increased to pay for all of the new prisons, guards, police, prosecutors and judges stand in your way.

Keep in mind that there is absolutely no chance of winning the war on drugs. Congress and the General Accounting Office have admitted as much; any sane person knows it. America could build prisons until they run out of bricks and bars and still there would be no foreseeable victory in the war on drugs.

As a closing thought, I, myself, am living proof that prison is not a deterrent to drug trafficking or drug abuse, nor will it ever be, no matter how lengthy the prison sentences become. Perhaps you may think my viewpoint is one of the prisoner minority? Don't bet on it. I've met thousands of drug traffickers and addicts in my life and I've never seen one go straight because he/she was worried about prison. The only feasible solution to the "drug-related crime," which is all caused by the *illegal* status of drugs, is to end drug prohibition to remove the *illicit* profit margin.

7

Legalization Would Help Solve the Nation's Drug Problem

Peter J. Riga

Peter J. Riga, a freelance writer and theologian, is an attorney in private practice in Houston, Texas.

The law-enforcement approach to America's drug problem has proven ineffective. Legalizing drugs would greatly reduce the prison population, making vast sums of money available for drug rehabilitation, a far more effective solution to the nation's drug problems. In addition, money raised through the legal sale of drugs could fund public education designed to combat drug abuse.

I practice law in the criminal courts of Harris County, Texas. I am constantly amazed that over half of the prisoners in the justice system are black and another third are Mexican or other minorities. All are poor. More than half of them are in prison because of drug-related crimes.

There are few whites in this group because drug crimes (possession, use, distribution, theft-robbery to get money for a habit, etc.) are mostly crimes of poor people, and whites have the money to buy drugs (legal and illegal), to pay for good lawyers, or to afford rehab centers. Moreover, the real drug of choice in the white community is alcohol. It is legal, available, and there are many programs to deal with its negative effects. To me it is shameful and irrational that users of cocaine and heroin are labeled criminals and go to jail—with almost no hope of therapy or rehab—while the users of the powerful drug alcohol are considered sick (alcoholics) and given therapy.

There are deep social causes for illegal drug use which our present law-enforcement strategy does almost nothing to alleviate. Up to 1980, social programs in the cities were beginning to show some progress, but with the Reagan administration's singular emphasis on law and order, these were radically curtailed. However, statistics from 1980 to 1992 on

Peter J. Riga, "The Drug War Is a Crime: Let's Try Decriminalization," *Commonweal*, July 16, 1993;

what came to be known as "the war on drugs" tell a grim tale. While over $100 billion was spent on the effort—an eightfold monetary increase—a 1990 report of the National Institute on Drug Abuse, Drug Enforcement Administration of the Department of Justice tells us that there are today 6 million hard-core, illegal-drug users, double the estimate in 1980. All told, each year 14 million Americans use illegal drugs for one reason or another. They spend about $50 billion on marijuana, cocaine, crack, heroin, and hallucinogens. While the number of deaths and murders connected to illegal drugs has soared to some 21,000 a year (they account for the highest number of deaths among minorities under the age of thirty-five), the figure nonetheless remains smaller than the number of deaths each year which result from drunk driving (22,000).

A colossal failure

If the war on drugs proves anything, it is that its emphasis on law enforcement—on the supply-side rather than the demand-side—has been a colossal failure. Yet the appointment of Lee P. Brown to a cabinet-level position as the Clinton administration's first director of the Office of National Drug Control Policy does not indicate a shift in emphasis. Brown's background is in law enforcement (he has headed police departments in New York, Atlanta, and Houston), and the initial Clinton budget ($13 billion) seems to be a carryover of previous spending patterns: the bulk of the money is earmarked for law enforcement, surveillance, prison construction, and border patrols, rather than education and rehabilitation. If we were to legalize and control the use of illegal drugs, we could make some significant progress. For starters, we could cut the prison population by more than half, thereby raising vast sums of money for proper law enforcement *and* therapy for those addicted. At present, treatment is available for only about 15 percent of the nation's drug addicts. The funding is just not there. Yet we are now spending about $159 a day to house a prisoner in one of our overcrowded jails. Instead of seeking to build more jails at enormous costs, we should apply a fraction of that money to drug rehab centers, a proven method of helping people get off drugs.

One of the reasons rampant crime is associated with drugs is the drug trade's great profitability. The money involved is so ready, so substantial, that dealers can always find another recruit to take the place of someone who has just been caught. For those imprisoned, for use or for dealing, incarceration does little more than harden them. It certainly doesn't rehabilitate them. They come out of prison only to involve themselves again, and this in turn accounts for the system's high recidivism rates.

Well-known facts

These facts are well known and yet we refuse to face them. We keep on going back to law enforcement and punishment, a costly and consistent failure. Fed up with mandatory sentencing guidelines, two prominent federal judges in New York recently refused to hear drug-related cases (*New York Times*, April 17, 1993). As another federal judge, Robert W. Sweet, told the *Times*, "The present policy of trying to prohibit the use of drugs through the use of criminal law is a mistake."

Let me hasten to say that neither the legalization of drugs nor the mere availability of treatment/rehabilitation would cure the root causes of their widespread use. In themselves, these are only palliatives. The real solution for challenging and changing the grip of the drug culture lies in people having some sense of hope for their future. A study in the 1950s traced adolescent heroin addiction in New York City. It found that the majority of users were from poor neighborhoods. Since then, numerous other studies have established the link between deprivation and drug use. The problem is not one of race, but of class and the sense of possibility.

Nevertheless, I think the time has come to legalize drugs. The legalization I envision would not be without regulation. Those who drive while under the influence of drugs would be severely dealt with—much as we do with those who drink and drive. Thanks to such groups as MADD [Mothers Against Drunk Driving], laws related to drunken driving have become tighter and more strictly enforced. We must do the same with other drugs. Part of the money from the legal sale of these drugs could be allocated for education and rehabilitation, much as we do with tax money from alcohol sales and from gambling.

If we were to legalize and control the use of illegal drugs, we could make some significant progress.

The real solution to drug addiction lies in individuals' heightened awareness of the destructiveness of drugs, and in self-pride programs for society's "have-nots." The United States has cut back drastically on its alcohol and tobacco consumption because people have become aware that even in moderation these legal products are dangerous. The same thing must be done for other drugs. Pragmatically, the legal and controlled sale of drugs would not only reduce crime but channel valuable resources into treatment. It is a risk, but given the alternatives, the risk is worth taking.

Drug legalization in England and Holland has had mixed results. While there has been a slight increase in drug use in those countries, the number of crimes associated with drugs has decreased. In the U.S. there are now eleven states which have decriminalized the personal use of marijuana. According to the National Institute on Drug Abuse, there has been no increase in its use in those states.

Clearly, there will be some increase in drug use if drugs are made legal and accessible at a reasonable price. Yet the benefits of legalization will outweigh the negatives: less crime, illegal profits, more resources available for greater rehabilitation efforts, fewer jail cells and prisoners, better utilization of law enforcement personnel, greater respect for law, fewer corrupted policemen, and fewer deaths from impure substances. Furthermore, taxes from these legalized drugs will fund treatment centers and educational outreach. If we can distribute condoms and clean needles to control the spread of disease, why can't we bring ourselves to distribute drugs cheaply and legally? The same arguments about cause and effect ought to be made here as well.

8
Drug Use Should Be Decriminalized

Elliott Currie

Elliott Currie is a research associate at the Institute for the Study of Social Change at the University of California at Berkeley. He is the author of Confronting Crime: An American Challenge *and* Reckoning: Drugs, the Cities, and the American Future.

Increased criminal justice efforts would not solve the problem of drug use in America. On the other hand, complete deregulation of the production, use, and sale of drugs would also prove ineffective. Rather than embracing either of these extreme tactics, the United States should decriminalize drug use while simultaneously emphasizing treatment, public health, and community safety.

One of the strongest implications of what we now know about the causes of endemic drug abuse is that the criminal-justice system's effect on the drug crisis will inevitably be limited. That shouldn't surprise us in the 1990s; it has, after all, been a central argument of drug research since the 1950s. Today, as the drug problem has worsened, the limits of the law are if anything even clearer. But that does not mean that the justice system has no role to play in a more effective strategy against drugs. Drugs will always be a "law-enforcement problem" in part, and the real job is to define what we want the police and the courts to accomplish.

We will never, for reasons that will shortly become clear, punish our way out of the drug crisis. We can, however, use the criminal-justice system, in small but significant ways, to improve the prospects of drug users who are now caught in an endless loop of court, jail, and street. And we can use law enforcement, in small but significant ways, to help strengthen the ability of drug-ridden communities to defend themselves against violence, fear, and demoralization. Today the criminal-justice system does very little of the first and not enough of the second. But doing these things well will require far-reaching changes in our priorities. Above all, we will have to shift from an approach in which discouraging drug use through punishment and fear takes central place to one that emphasizes three very

Elliott Currie, "Toward a Policy on Drugs: Decriminalization? Legalization?" *Dissent*, Winter 1993, adapted from *Reckoning: Drugs, the Cities, and the American Future* by Elliott Currie.

different principles: the reintegration of drug abusers into productive life, the reduction of harm, and the promotion of community safety.

This is a tall order, but, as we shall see, something similar is being practiced in many countries that suffer far less convulsing drug problems than we do. Their experience suggests that a different and more humane criminal-justice response to drugs is both possible and practical. Today, there is much debate about the role of the justice system in a rational drug policy—but for the most part, the debate is between those who would intensify the effort to control drugs through the courts and prisons and those who want to take drugs out of the orbit of the justice system altogether. I do not think that either approach takes sufficient account of the social realities of drug abuse; and both, consequently, exaggerate the role of regulatory policies in determining the shape and seriousness of the problem. But those are not the only alternatives. In between, there is a range of more promising strategies—what some Europeans call a "third way"—that is more attuned to those realities and more compatible with our democratic values.

Escalation will not work

One response to the failure of the drug war has been to call for more of what we've already done—even harsher sentences, still more money for jails and prisons—on the grounds that we have simply not provided enough resources to fight the war effectively. That position was shared by the Bush administration and many Democrats in Congress as well. But the strategy of upping the ante cannot work; and even to attempt it on a large scale would dramatically increase the social costs that an over-reliance on punishment has already brought. We've seen that the effort to contain the drug problem through force and fear has already distorted our justice system in fundamental ways and caused a rippling of secondary costs throughout the society as a whole. Much more of this would alter the character of American society beyond recognition. And it would not solve the drug problem.

Why wouldn't more of the same do the job?

To understand why escalating the war on drugs would be unlikely to make much difference—short of efforts on a scale that would cause unprecedented social damage—we need to consider how the criminal-justice system is, in theory, *supposed* to work to reduce drug abuse and drug-related crime. Criminologists distinguish between two mechanisms by which punishment may decrease illegal behavior. One is "incapacitation," an unlovely term that simply means that locking people up will keep them—as long as they are behind bars—from engaging in the behavior we wish to suppress. The other is "deterrence," by which we mean either that people tempted to engage in the behavior will be persuaded otherwise by the threat of punishment ("general deterrence"), or that individuals, once punished, will be less likely to engage in the behavior again ("specific deterrence"). What makes the drug problem so resistant to even very heavy doses of criminalization is that neither mechanism works effectively for most drug offenders—particularly those most heavily involved in the drug subcultures of the street.

The main reason why incapacitation is unworkable as a strategy against drug offenders is that there are so many of them that a serious attempt to put them all—or even just the "hard core"—behind bars is unrealistic, even in the barest fiscal terms. This is obvious if we pause to recall the sheer number of people who use hard drugs in the United States. Consider the estimates of the number of people who have used drugs during the previous year provided annually by the NIDA (National Institute on Drug Abuse) Household Survey—which substantially *understates* the extent of hard-drug use. Even if we exclude the more than 20 million people who used marijuana in the past year, the number of hard-drug users is enormous: the survey estimates over six million cocaine users in 1991 (including over a million who used crack), about 700,000 heroin users, and 5.7 million users of hallucinogens and inhalants. Even if we abandon the aim of imprisoning less serious hard-drug users, thus allowing the most conservative accounting of the costs of incapacitation, the problem remains staggering: by the lowest estimates, there are no fewer than two million hard-core abusers of cocaine and heroin alone.

If we take as a rough approximation that about 25 percent of America's prisoners are behind bars for drug offenses, that gives us roughly 300,000 drug offenders in prison at any given point—and this after several years of a hugely implemented war mainly directed at lower-level dealers and street drug users. We have seen what this flood of offenders has done to the nation's courts and prisons, but what is utterly sobering is that even this massive effort at repression has barely scratched the surface: according to the most optimistic estimate, we may at any point be incarcerating on drug-related charges about one-eighth of the country's hard-core cocaine and heroin abusers. And where drug addiction is truly endemic, the disparity is greater. By 1989 there were roughly 20,000 drug offenders on any given day in New York State's prisons, but there were an estimated 200,000 to 250,000 *heroin* addicts in New York City alone. To be sure, these figures obscure the fact that many prisoners behind bars for *non*drug offenses are also hard-core drug users; but the figures are skewed in the other direction by the large (if unknown) number of active drug dealers who are not themselves addicted.

We've seen that the effort to contain the drug problem through force and fear has already distorted our justice system in fundamental ways.

Thus, though we cannot quantify these proportions with any precision, the basic point should be clear: the pool of *serious* addicts and active dealers is far, far larger than the numbers we now hold in prison—even in the midst of an unprecedented incarceration binge that has made us far and away the world's leader in imprisonment rates.

What would it mean to expand our prison capacity enough to put the *majority* of hard-core users and dealers behind bars for long terms? To triple the number of users and low-level dealers behind bars, even putting two drug offenders to a cell, would require about 300,000 new cells. At a conservative estimate of about $100,000 per cell, that means a $30 billion investment in construction alone. If we then assume an equally conservative estimate of about $25,000 in yearly operating costs per inmate, we add roughly $15 billion a year to our current costs. Yet this would leave the majority of drug dealers and hard-core addicts still on the streets and, of course, would do nothing to prevent new ones from emerging in otherwise unchanged communities to take the place of those behind bars.

It is not entirely clear, moreover, what that huge expenditure would, in fact, accomplish. For if the goal is to prevent the drug dealing and other crimes that addicts commit, the remedy may literally cost more than the disease. Although drug addicts do commit a great deal of crime, most of them are very minor ones, mainly petty theft and small-time drug dealing. This pattern has been best illuminated in the study of Harlem heroin addicts by Bruce Johnson and his co-workers. Most of the street addicts in this study were "primarily thieves and small-scale drug distributors who avoided serious crimes, like robbery, burglary, assault." The average income per nondrug crime among these addicts was $35. Even among the most criminally active group—what these researchers called "robber-dealers"—the annual income from crime amounted on average to only about $21,000, and for the great majority—about 70 percent—of less active addict-criminals, it ranged from $5,000 to $13,000. At the same time, the researchers estimated that the average cost per day of confining one addict in a New York City jail cell was roughly $100, or $37,000 a year. Putting these numbers together, Johnson and his co-workers came to the startling conclusion that it would cost considerably more to lock up all of Harlem's street addicts than to simply let them continue to "take care of business" on the street.

Legalization

If we cannot expect much from intensified criminalization, would the legalization of hard drugs solve the drug crisis?

No: it would not. To understand why, we need to consider the claims for legalization's effects in the light of what we know about the roots and meanings of endemic drug abuse. First, however, we need to step back in order to sort out exactly what we *mean* by "legalization"—a frustratingly vague and often confused term that means very different things to different interpreters. Many, indeed, who argue most vehemently one way or the other about the merits of legalization are not really clear just what it is they are arguing *about*.

At one end of the spectrum are those who mean by legalization the total deregulation of the production, sale, and use of all drugs—hard and soft. Advocates of this position run the gamut from right-wing economists to some staunch liberals, united behind the principle that government has no business interfering in individuals' choice to ingest whatever substances they desire. Most who subscribe to that general view would add several qualifiers: for example, that drugs (like alcohol) should not be sold to minors, or that drug advertising should be regulated or prohibited, or (less often) that drugs should be sold only in government-run stores, as alcohol is in some states. But these are seen as necessary, if sometimes grudging, exceptions to the general rule that private drug transactions should not be the province of government intervention. For present purposes, I will call this the "free-market" approach to drug control, and describe its central aim as the "deregulation" of the drug market.

Another approach would not go so far as to deregulate the drug trade, but would opt for the controlled dispensation of drugs to addicts who have been certified by a physician, under strict guidelines as to amounts and conditions of use. Something like this "medical model," in varying forms, guided British policy toward heroin after the 1920s. Under the so-called British system, addicts could receive heroin from physicians or clinics—but the private production and distribution of heroin was always subject to strong penalties, as was the use of the drug except in its medical or "pharmaceutical" form. (A small-scale experiment in cocaine prescription is presently being tried in the city of Liverpool.) Since the seventies, the British have largely abandoned prescribing heroin in favor of methadone—a synthetic opiate that blocks the body's craving for heroin but, among other things, produces less of a pleasurable "high" and lasts considerably longer. The practice of dispensing methadone to heroin addicts came into wide use in the United States in the 1960s and remains a major form of treatment. Methadone prescription, of course, does not "legalize" heroin, and the possession or sale of methadone itself is highly illegal outside of the strictly controlled medical relationship.

Still another meaning sometimes given to legalization is what is more accurately called the "decriminalization" of drug *use*. We may continue to define the production and sale of certain drugs as crimes and subject them to heavy penalties, but not punish those who only *use* the drugs (or have small amounts in their possession), or punish them very lightly—with small fines, for example, rather than jail. Something close to this is the practice in Holland, which is often wrongly perceived as a country that has legalized drugs. Though drug use remains technically illegal, Dutch policy is to focus most law-enforcement resources on sales, especially on larger traffickers, while dealing with users mainly through treatment programs and other social services, rather than the police and courts.

Many . . . who argue most vehemently one way or the other about the merits of legalization are not really clear just what it is they are arguing about.

Another aspect of Dutch policy illustrates a further possible meaning of legalization: we may selectively decriminalize *some* drugs, in some amounts, and not others. The Dutch, in practice—though not in law—have tolerated both sale and use of small amounts of marijuana and hashish, but not heroin or cocaine. A German court has recently ruled that possession of small amounts of hashish and marijuana is not a crime, and, indeed, marijuana possession has largely been decriminalized in some American states, though usually as a matter of practical policy rather than legislation.

Let me make my own view clear. I think much would be gained if we followed the example of some European countries and moved toward decriminalization of the drug user. I also think there is a strong argument for treating marijuana differently from the harder drugs, and that there is room for careful experiment with strictly controlled medical prescription for some addicts. For reasons that will become clear, decriminalization is not a panacea; it will not end the drug crisis, but it could substantially decrease the irrationality and inhumanity of our present punitive war on drugs.

The free-market approach, on the other hand, is another matter entirely. Some variant of that approach is more prominent in drug-policy debates in the United States than in other developed societies, probably because it meshes with a strongly individualistic and antigovernment political culture. Indeed, the degree to which the debate over drug policy has been dominated by the clash between fervent drug "warriors" and equally ardent free-market advocates is a peculiarly American phenomenon. Much of that clash is about philosophical principles, and addressing those issues in detail would take more space than we have. My aim here is simply to examine the empirical claims of the free-market perspective in the light of what we know about the social context of drug abuse. Here the free-market view fails to convince. It greatly exaggerates the benefits of deregulation while simultaneously underestimating the potential costs.

There is no question that the criminalization of drugs produces negative secondary consequences—especially in the unusually punitive form that criminalization has taken in the United States. Nor is there much question that this argues for a root-and-branch rethinking of our current punitive strategy—to which we'll return later—especially our approach to drug *users*.

But proponents of full-scale deregulation of hard drugs also tend to gloss over the very real primary costs of drug abuse—particularly on the American level—and to exaggerate the degree to which the multiple pathologies surrounding drug use in America are simply an unintended result of a "prohibitionist" regulatory policy. No country now legalizes the sale of hard drugs. Yet no other country has anything resembling the American drug problem. That alone should tell us that more than prohibition is involved in shaping the magnitude and severity of our drug crisis. But there is more technical evidence as well. It confirms that much (though, of course, not all) of the harm caused by endemic drug abuse is intrinsic to the impact of hard drugs themselves (and the street cultures in which drug abuse is embedded) within the context of a glaringly unequal, depriving, and deteriorating society. And it affirms that we will not substantially reduce that harm without attacking the social roots of the extraordinary demand for hard drugs in the United States. Just as we cannot punish our way out of the drug crisis, neither will we escape its grim toll by deregulating the drug market.

Violence and addiction

The most important argument for a free-market approach has traditionally been that it would reduce or eliminate the crime and violence now inextricably entwined with addiction to drugs and with the drug trade. In this view it is precisely the illegality of drug use that is responsible for drug-related crime—which, in turn, is seen as by far the largest part of the overall problem of urban violence. Criminal sanctions against drugs, as one observer insists, "cause the bulk of murders and property crime in major urban areas." Because criminalization makes drugs far more costly than they would otherwise be, addicts are forced to commit crimes in order to gain enough income to afford their habits. Moreover, they are forced to seek out actively criminal people in order to obtain their drugs, which exposes them to even more destructive criminal influences. At the same time, the fact that the drug trade is illegal means both that it is hugely profitable and that the inevitable conflicts and disputes over "turf" or between dealers and users cannot be resolved or moderated by legal mechanisms, and hence are usually resolved by violence.

For all of these reasons, it is argued, outlawing drugs has the unintended, but inevitable, effect of causing a flood of crime and urban violence that would not exist otherwise and sucking young people, especially, into a bloody drug trade. If we legalize the sale and use of hard drugs, the roots of drug-related violence would be severed, and much of the larger crisis of criminal violence in the cities would disappear.

I think much would be gained if we followed the example of some European countries and moved toward decriminalization of the drug user.

But the evidence suggests that although this view contains an element of truth, it is far too simplistic—and that it relies on stereotypical assumptions about the relationship between drugs and crime that have been called into serious question since the classic drug research of the 1950s. In particular, the widely held notion that most of the crime committed by addicts can be explained by their need for money to buy illegal drugs does not fit well with the evidence.

In its popular form, the drugs-cause-crime argument is implicitly based on the assumption that addict crime is caused by pharmacological compulsion—as a recent British study puts it, on a kind of "enslavement" model in which the uncontrollable craving for drugs forces an otherwise law-abiding citizen to engage in crime for gain. As we've seen, however, a key finding of most of the research into the meaning of drug use and the growth of drug subcultures since the 1950s has been that the purely pharmacological craving for drugs is by no means the most important motive for drug use. Nor is it clear that those cravings are typically so uncontrollable that addicts are in any meaningful sense "driven" to crime to satisfy them.

On the surface, there is much to suggest a strong link between crime and the imperatives of addiction. The studies of addict crime by John Ball and Douglas Anglin and their colleagues show not only that the most heavily addicted commit huge numbers of crimes, but also that their crime rates seem to increase when their heroin use increases and to fall when it declines. Thus, for example, heroin addicts in Ball's study in Baltimore had an average of 255 "crime days" per year when they were actively addicted, versus about 65 when they were not. In general, the level of property crime appears in these studies to go up simultaneously with increasing intensity of drug use. One explanation, and perhaps the most common one, is that the increased need for money to buy drugs drives addicts into more crime.

But a closer look shows that things are considerably more complicated. To begin with, it is a recurrent finding that most people who both abuse drugs and commit crimes began committing the crimes *before* they began using drugs—meaning that their need for drugs cannot have caused their initial criminal involvement (though it may have accelerated it later). George Vaillant's follow-up study of addicts and alcoholics found, for example, that, unlike alcoholics, heroin addicts had typically been involved in delinquency and crime well before they began their career of substance abuse. While alcoholics seemed to become involved in crime as a *result* of their abuse of alcohol, more than half of the heroin addicts (versus just 5 percent of the alcoholics) "were known to have been delinquent *before* drug abuse." A federal survey of drug use among prison inmates in 1986, similarly, found that three-fifths of those who had ever used a "major drug" regularly—that is, heroin, cocaine, methadone, PCP, or LSD—had not done so until after their first arrest.

Other studies have found that for many addicts, drug use and crime seem to have begun more or less *independently* without one clearly causing the other. This was the finding, for example, in Charles Faupel and Carl Klockars's study of hard-core heroin addicts in Wilmington, Delaware. "All of our respondents," they note, "reported some criminal activity prior to their first use of heroin." Moreover, "perhaps most importantly, virtually all of our respondents reported that they believed that their criminal and drug careers began independently of one another, although both careers became intimately interconnected as each evolved."

Just as we cannot punish our way out of the drug crisis, neither will we escape its grim toll by deregulating the drug market.

More recent research shows that the drugs-crime relationship may be even more complex than this suggests. It is not only that crime may precede drug use, especially heavy or addictive use, or that both may emerge more or less independently; it is also likely that there are several *different* kinds of drugs-crime connections among different types of drug users. David Nurco of the University of Maryland and his colleagues, for example, studying heroin addicts in Baltimore and New York City, found that nine different kinds of addicts could be distinguished by the type and severity of their crimes. Like earlier researchers, they found that most addicts committed large numbers of crimes—mainly drug dealing and small-scale property crime, notably shoplifting, burglary, and fencing. Others were involved in illegal gambling and what the researchers called "deception crimes"—including forgery and con games—and a relatively small percentage had engaged in violent crime. On the whole, addicts heavily involved in one type of crime were not likely to be involved in others; as the researchers put it, they tended to be either "dealers or stealers," but rarely both. About 6 percent of the addicts, moreover, were "uninvolved"—they did not commit crimes either while addicted or before, or during periods of nonaddiction interspersed in the course of their longer addiction careers.

The most troubling group of addicts—what the researchers called "violent generalists"—were only about 7 percent of the total sample, but they were extremely active—and very dangerous; they accounted for over half of all the violent crimes committed by the entire sample. Moreover, revealingly, the violent generalists were very active in serious crime *before* they became addicted to narcotics as well as during periods of nonaddiction thereafter—again demonstrating that the violence was not dependent on their addiction itself. Nurco and his colleagues measured the addicts' criminal activity by what they called "crime days" per year. Addicts were asked how many days they had committed each of several types of crime; since on any given day they might have committed more than one type of crime, the resulting figure could add up to more than the number of days in the year. The violent generalists averaged an astonishing 900 crime days a year over the course of their careers. The rates were highest during periods when they were heavily addicted to drugs. But even *before* they were addicted, they averaged 573 crime days, and 491 after their addiction had ended. Indeed, the most active group of violent generalists engaged in more crime *prior* to addiction than any other group did *while* addicted. And they continued to commit crimes—often violent ones—long after they had ceased to be addicted to narcotics.

None of this is to deny that serious addiction to heroin or other illegal drugs can accelerate the level of crime among participants in the drug culture, or stimulate crime even in some users who are otherwise not criminal. Higher levels of drug use *do* go hand in hand with increased crime, especially property crime. Certainly, many addicts mug, steal, or sell their bodies for drugs. The point is that—as the early drug researchers discovered in the 1950s—both crime and drug abuse tend to be spawned by the same set of unfavorable social circumstances, and they interact with one another in much more complex ways than the simple addiction-leads-to-crime view proposes. Simply providing drugs more easily to people enmeshed in the drug cultures of the cities is not likely to cut the deep social roots of addict crime.

Both crime and drug abuse tend to be spawned by the same set of unfavorable social circumstances.

If we take the harms of drug abuse seriously, and I think we must, we cannot avoid being deeply concerned about anything that would significantly increase the availability of hard drugs within the American social context; and no one seriously doubts that legalization would indeed increase availability, and probably lower prices for many drugs. In turn, increased availability—as we know from the experience with alcohol—typically leads to increased consumption, and with it increased social and public-health costs. A growing body of research, for example, shows that most alcohol-related health problems, including deaths from cirrhosis and other diseases, were far lower during Prohibition than afterward, when per capita alcohol consumption rose dramatically (by about 75 percent, for example, between 1950 and 1980). It is difficult to imagine why a similar rise in consumption—and in the associated public-health problems—would not follow the full-scale legalization of cocaine, heroin, methamphetamine, and PCP (not to mention the array of as yet undiscovered "designer" drugs that a legalized corporate drug industry would be certain to develop).

If consumption increased, it would almost certainly increase most among the strata already most vulnerable to hard-drug use—thus exacerbating the social stratification of the drug crisis. It is among the poor and near-poor that offsetting measures like education and drug treatment are least effective and where the countervailing social supports and opportunities are least strong. We would expect, therefore, that a free-market policy applied to hard drugs would produce the same results it has created with the *legal* killer drugs, tobacco and alcohol—namely, a widening disparity in use between the better-off and the disadvantaged. And that disparity is already stunning. According to a recent study by Colin McCord and Howard Freeman of Harlem Hospital, between 1979 and 1981—that is, *before* the crack epidemic of the eighties—Harlem blacks were 283 times as likely to die of drug dependency as whites in the general population. Drug deaths, combined with deaths from cirrhosis, alcoholism, cardiovascular disease, and homicide, helped to give black men in Harlem a shorter life expectancy than men in Bangladesh. That is the social reality that the rather abstract calls for the legalization of hard-drug sales tend to ignore.

9
Drugs Should Not Be Legalized

William J. Olson

William J. Olson is a senior fellow at the National Strategy Information Center, a Washington, D.C., organization that formulates policy on national defense and security issues. He was formerly the deputy assistant secretary of state in the Bureau of International Narcotics Matters at the Department of State.

Since the late 1980s, calls to legalize drugs have become more frequent. Among other arguments, legalizers base their appeals on the following faulty assertions: prohibiting drugs causes crime, interdiction has failed, and drug use harms no one and is a private issue. Americans should resist these arguments and should continue to support antidrug measures.

Americans are again being asked to legalize drugs. Support for a review of drug legalization has come from a broad range of public figures, from former U.S. surgeon general Joycelyn Elders, the popular Baltimore mayor Kurt Schmoke, conservative pundits, academics, leading economists, experienced foreign officials, and individuals in the press.

The call for legalization has had a new lease on life because the Clinton Administration is signaling ambivalence on drug issues, but policy makers should pause and ponder the consequences of such a dramatic reversal in public policy. As social scientist Charles Murray indicates, there is a fundamental conflict between freedom and responsibility implicit in the issue of legalization.

> I cannot bring myself to support a federal law legalizing drugs . . . as a single, isolated change in social policy. For though I am confident that legalization would work in a society where people are held responsible for the consequences of their actions, that's not the way contemporary America works. . . . To legalize drugs in America as of 1990 is to give people the right to be responsible for themselves without also obliging them to do so.[1]

There are three basic reasons why the idea of legalization once again

William J. Olson, "Why Americans Should Resist the Legalization of Drugs," Heritage Foundation *Backgrounder*, July 18, 1994. Reprinted by permission of The Heritage Foundation, ©1994.

has begun to attract interest.

First, a small and influential group of opinion makers, especially those close to policy makers, have been able to advance a policy agenda that the majority may oppose.

Second, some appointees in the Clinton Administration and other public officials now favor some form of legalization. Even though Joycelyn Elders, for example, represents a tiny minority, because her views are magnified by press coverage they have set much of the tone for the national debate on drugs. Moreover, the President's one-time, half-hearted rebuttal of Elders never carried moral conviction and was not backed by clear policy. So her words carried more weight. In fact, on drug enforcement, the Clinton Administration generally is ambivalent and lacks coherence or direction.[2]

Several questionable assumptions underlie the arguments for legalization.

Third, there is a feeling that the worst may be over and that it is time to relax legal restrictions against drug use. In 1993, the University of Michigan High School Senior Survey, one of the nation's largest annual drug surveys, reported that declines in adolescent use of illegal drugs in recent years were holding. Significantly, this research indicated that perceptions of risk and peer norms, not the availability of drugs, led to declines in use.

But the survey also noted that attitudes among younger students, particularly eighth- and ninth-graders, who were not hearing any coherent social message about the risks of using drugs, were drifting back to an earlier view that experimenting with illegal drugs was not so bad. The 1994 survey confirms this pattern. In addition, the major survey of hospital emergency room admissions for 1993 shows increases in admissions for drug-related emergencies. These are warning signs—not a confirmed trend, but a series of flashing lights.

Forced to deal at first hand with the consequences of virtual legalization in the 1960s and 1970s, Americans reacted strongly by demanding action to stop crime and drug trafficking on America's streets. That mood has not changed. Officials and pundits who wish to change public attitudes on this issue need to marshal better arguments and stronger evidence to support the case for drug legalization than they have mustered thus far. The most fashionable arguments do not begin to make a valid case for such a momentous change in public policy.

Members of Congress, state legislators, and ordinary Americans following the legalization debate should keep certain points in mind in this debate. For one thing, there is no single argument for legalization; advocates use an assortment of arguments, many of them contradictory. This viewpoint presents a distilled but representative range of these pro-legalization arguments. Several assumptions underlie these arguments, and these assumptions are presented in their starkest form in order to make them clear and explicit. For another, the issue cannot be resolved simply by an appeal to undisputed interpretations of the data. Moreover, several questionable assumptions underlie the arguments for legalization. Once these assumptions are analyzed and rejected, the case for drug legalization is severely weakened.

The faulty logic of legalization

Some Americans have long favored immediate legalization of all illegal drugs, particularly marijuana, cocaine, and heroin. Others, such as the editors of *High Times* and the National Organization for the Reform of Marijuana Laws (NORML), have focused on the legalization of cannabis as just another lifestyle choice. But these views are marginal to the current debate on drug legalization.[3] More important are the views of "mainstream advocates" of drug legalization, most of whom are prepared to acknowledge that drug abuse is bad for individuals and society but still believe that legalization in some form would be good public policy. Thus, public personalities as different in their views as former surgeon general Joycelyn Elders, *National Review* editor-at-large William F. Buckley, Nobel economist Milton Friedman, and Baltimore mayor Kurt Schmoke have argued for some degree of legalization. To weigh today's campaign for legalization, lawmakers must explore the views of these influential advocates.

Seven main arguments are used to justify legalization. Though not every advocate uses every argument and not everyone who does use them advocates legalization *per se*, all seven figure one way or another in the rationale for legalization. These arguments are:

1. The prohibition of drugs only leads to more crime.
2. Interdiction has failed.
3. Society cannot afford the costs of imprisoning drug offenders; enforcement falls disproportionately on minorities, and the cost exceeds the benefits.
4. Drug use is not that bad.
5. Society permits alcohol and tobacco use, which kills many more Americans.
6. The drug problem is primarily a treatment issue. In addition, policy should focus on demand reduction.
7. In a democracy, the government has no right to interfere in the private lives of citizens if their activities harm nobody else.

Incorporating all seven of these converging propositions, implicitly or explicitly, is the general argument that because society has no right to control private drug use, it cannot do so effectively. The only proper conclusion from this argument, it is claimed, is legalization, whether it be absolute legalization (all drugs should be legalized for all individuals), which is a distinctly minority view, or some form of controlled legalization (drugs would not be made available to everyone who wanted them, such as those below a certain age), the most common position.

Argument 1: Prohibition cannot work and encourages crime. Americans are painfully familiar with the experience of prohibition. Against the backdrop of Eliot Ness battling Al Capone, the social experiment of trying to control alcohol consumption is seen as a dismal failure. By analogy, it is claimed that any effort to control any other drug must be doomed to the same fate. So the alternative must be to legalize drugs; not to do so means more opportunities for criminals and ineffective policies which punish innocent victims with draconian laws.

The most impressive spokesman for this point of view is Nobel laureate Milton Friedman, according to whom, "Drugs are a tragedy for addicts. But criminalizing their use converts that tragedy into a disaster for society. . . . Our experience with the prohibition of drugs is a replay of our experience with the prohibition of alcoholic beverages." Friedman maintains that had cocaine been legalized in 1972, there would have been no crack epidemic because crack would not have been invented and there would be far fewer addicts. "The lives of thousands, perhaps hundreds of thousands of innocent victims would have been saved. . . . The ghettos of our major cities would not be drug-and-crime-infested no-man's lands. Fewer people would be in jails, and fewer jails would have been built." Moreover, adds Friedman, "Colombia, Bolivia and Peru would not be suffering from narco-terror, and we would not be distorting our foreign policy. . . ." The answer is to decriminalize drugs and treat addicts, which is more humane than seeking to punish them:

> Decriminalization would not prevent us from treating drugs as we now treat alcohol and tobacco: prohibiting sales of drugs to minors, outlawing the advertising of drugs and similar measures. Such measures could be enforced, while outright prohibition cannot be. Moreover, if even a small fraction of the money we now spend on trying to enforce drug prohibition were devoted to treatment and rehabilitation, in an atmosphere of compassion not punishment, the reduction in drug usage and in the harm done to users could be dramatic.[4]

Thus, to paraphrase Friedman, with legalization, drug use will drop, crime will be reduced, and Americans will be better off with more money in their pockets. According to this view, prohibition has caused immense harm, and the solution is decriminalization. Professor Friedman's view best represents what may be called the "prohibition-cannot-work" school. Many others, some marshalling considerable facts about the failure of alcohol prohibition, use this putative analogy to suggest the futility of any prohibition against drugs.

The foundation of Friedman's argument rests on the failed experiment with the prohibition of alcohol and the validity of the analogy between alcohol and illegal drugs. But interpreting the experience of prohibition in the 1920s and 1930s is not as simple as is usually assumed. The Eighteenth Amendment to the Constitution did not make alcohol consumption illegal; it prohibited the manufacture, sale, importation, or transportation of intoxicating liquors. But because the law did not prohibit consumption, it contained an inconsistency which it could never overcome: It made alcohol illegal to produce but left it legal to drink. A more consonant policy doubtless would have been less ambiguous in its intent and no doubt more effective in its results. The equivalent of prohibition today, with respect to drugs, would be to make drug use legal but to prosecute suppliers.

Despite this inconsistency, prohibition did have a positive effect. Alcohol consumption declined during the years of prohibition by between 30 percent and 50 percent, a significant change given alcohol's 5,000-year history of social acceptance and sanction. Alcohol-related deaths from cirrhosis declined sharply. Mental hospital admissions from alcohol-induced psychosis declined by 50 percent. And overall violent crimes did not increase, despite sharp increases before prohibition. Nor did prohibition create organized crime, which existed well before the Eighteenth Amendment or the Volstead Act.[5] It did give organized crime a boost, of course, but was not decisive in its creation or survival. A careful examination of the evidence concerning the effects of prohibition may not settle the issue, but the claims that prohibition was a complete failure are not based on historical facts. Too often, proponents of drug legalization ignore the historical facts and rely on myths about prohibition to make their case.

The experience of alcohol prohibition, moreover, is not in any case a fitting analogy for drawing conclusions about drug prohibition.[6] Alcohol, for better or worse, has a long heritage of social acceptance, and there is now considerable evidence that small amounts have some health benefits. Further, alcohol is safe for most people in small amounts and can be self-administered with a strong likelihood of self-control even over a lifetime of use. No similar claims can be made for psychoactive drugs, not even marijuana. This is not to deny, of course, that abuse of alcohol does untold damage to individuals and costs society enormous sums in health care and lost production.

Unlike alcohol, major illegal drugs such as heroin and cocaine have no long history of social acceptance. An overwhelming 80 percent or more of the public supports keeping these drugs illegal. These drugs are products of modern chemistry, being concentrates of naturally occurring substances. They also are far more powerful than alcohol, have stronger effects on users, are more destructive of personality, and are more addictive. The tradition that advocates of legalization must overcome is the public's unwillingness to accept legalization as a positive good. Since no one, including Professor Friedman, argues that drug addiction is desirable, it makes no sense to legalize substances that will cause yet more harm when overwhelming public support for their prohibition already exists. In this respect, the analogy to alcohol simply fails.

But prohibition of illegal drugs, legalization advocates argue, only supports the growth and spread of organized crime and violent street crime. Alcohol prohibition created the Mafia, the argument goes, and drug prohibition has created and deepens the influence and effects of drug cartels and crime in general.[7] Even if this indictment were true, which it is not, it would not justify the conclusion that society must quit trying to control drugs.

Crime and drugs

The case for a causal connection between prohibition and organized crime or crime in general is not persuasive.

In the first place, organized crime in America was not created by alcohol prohibition. Crime has prospered in many conditions without the boost attributed to prohibition, here and elsewhere.

Second, despite the claims that prohibition increases the profitability of controlled items, thus creating better opportunities and smarter organizations, no one has convincingly shown a causal link between prohibition and the growth of organized crime. Alcohol prohibition certainly increased the chances for profits, but organized or individual crime is opportunistic. Criminals will exploit any illegal avenue to increase profits. To claim that prohibition creates crime and that crime and criminals largely would disappear if drugs were legalized is interesting but hardly convincing.[8]

Third, the voluminous research on the relationship between violent crime and drugs does not indicate a causal link between legalizing drugs and stopping crime. Many criminals use drugs, and some drugs exacerbate violent tendencies. And a significant number of criminals committed crimes before they used them, not because they used them.[9] They do not become model citizens with legalized drugs. Some addicts resort to property crimes and violent crimes to sustain their habits. There is no evidence, however, that legalizing drugs would suddenly change all this. In the Netherlands, where drug use in certain areas is legal, property crime by addicts remains high. Unless drugs are distributed free of charge, at some point the addict is unable to earn an income and must resort to crime or panhandling to finance the habit. And the behavioral side effects of taking a drug do not disappear if the drug is made legal. If drug use increases with legalization, legalizing drugs is far more likely to create more crime, not less.

Fourth, the analogy between alcohol prohibition and experience with the prohibition of heroin and cocaine will not survive close scrutiny. Most areas of major opium production have no meaningful prohibition but still experience drug gangs. The Burmese government, for example, exercises no or only intermittent authority in most growing areas in what is the world's largest opium-producing region; and since most of the opium is consumed locally, prohibition on use, which is similarly lax, is not a major factor either. These areas are dominated by local warlords, who created themselves from opium profits and local nationalist sentiments, not from prohibition.

Too often, proponents of drug legalization ignore the historical facts and rely on myths about prohibition to make their case.

In the case of cocaine, awareness of the extent of the problem did not catch up with reality until production was on a massive scale in Bolivia, Colombia, and Peru and the cartels were deeply entrenched and well-financed. Although production and use were illegal in the United States and in the Andes, there was no real control of production at source and only pitiful efforts at interdiction and enforcement in the United States until cocaine wars and addiction exploded on American streets. It was the introduction of crack cocaine in 1986, and the death of young Maryland basketball star Len Bias, that aroused the public and led to the Reagan Administration's vigorous counter-drug policies and enforcement. The problem of organized crime in drugs *preceded* any real attempt at control.

For the sake of argument, however, let us assume a causal relationship between prohibition of substance and a rise in crime. Let us further assume that this relationship proceeds the way legalization advocates would have it: that prohibition creates crime and not the reverse. Does it necessarily follow that society is wrong to continue efforts that do not resolve the problem and may even make it worse? Not unless one believes that drug use and its consequences are acceptable in the first place and that any effort to control them is inherently wrong.

If drug use increases with legalization, legalizing drugs is far more likely to create more crime, not less.

Here an analogy will help to illustrate that prohibition, even if it fails or makes the problem worse, can be useful and necessary. There is a worldwide market for counterfeit airplane parts, and there also is a universal prohibition on making and selling them. This prohibition has not stopped their manufacture or sale; instead, it has made production far more lucrative. As one would expect, the result is more illegal parts. The view that forbidden fruit only makes matters worse leads to the conclusion that, since prohibition has failed and seemingly has made the situation worse, legalizing counterfeit parts is an acceptable solution. By this analogy, we should legalize counterfeit parts and be willing to fly in planes that carried them. The fact that we do not indicates that there is another value at work other than simply legalizing difficult problems.

In fact, society retains a right, and in many cases an obligation, to sustain programs that only reduce—but do not eliminate—the problems they are designed to resolve. This is true with respect to pollution, violent crime, child abuse, and countless other areas where there is no hope of ultimate success in ending the abuse. Many legalization advocates recognize this when dealing with other social issues, but apparently not when it comes to drugs.

In the case of drug control, absolute success is not necessary to justify prohibition, nor is an unpleasant side-effect necessarily sufficient cause to end it. Too many advocates of legalization argue that anything less than a Stakhanovite performance [one that surpasses expectations] in ending drug production, smuggling, and use is proof that decriminalization is the only appropriate response, but such an argument is not sustainable in any other area of social policy. After several thousand years, civilized societies have failed to eliminate murder, rape, or child abuse. Nor have they eliminated organized crime, the manufacture of counterfeit airplane parts, or genocide, but no one seriously sees these failures as justification for surrender.

Is there something inherent in drug use that sets it apart from all other behavior subject to social control? Perhaps so. In the meantime, however, complete success is not a justifiable criterion for judging the success or failure of prohibition, the admissibility of social controls, and the need to decriminalize drugs.

Argument 2: Interdiction has failed. Closely allied to the anti-prohibitionist argument is the view that because efforts to stop the flow of drugs have failed and are bound to fail, and because interdiction strategies have distorted American foreign policy and put allied countries needlessly at risk, America must discard this hopeless effort. Drugs, after all, continue to flow. The conclusion: the U.S. government should stop trying to do the impossible.

Mathea Falco, assistant secretary of state for international narcotics matters during the Carter Administration, makes this point in her book, *The Making of a Drug-Free America*, to justify a treatment-focused policy. "Not only have we failed to reduce the supplies of illicit drugs," says Falco, "we have also failed to reduce the human toll of our drug problem. Record numbers of arrests have not diminished violent crime, addiction, and urban blight."[10] The implication here is that all these problems are the result of drugs, a claim made by many others.

Her conclusion: stop interdiction efforts or at least focus on treatment and demand reduction in order to create a drug-free America. The putative failure to stop the flow of illegal drugs, however, by itself, does not justify foregoing interdiction. Most arguments against interdiction seem to assume that 100 percent success is the only justification for such a policy.[11] In any other context, this would be absurd.

The most common indictment of interdiction is that, despite heroic efforts, it has not cut off the flow of drugs or reduced appreciably their street price, but this indictment succeeds only by removing interdiction from its context and pretending that it must stand alone. In the best of all possible worlds, in which positive actions produce only expected results, price and availability would be sufficient as a basis for judgment. But the world is less than perfect, and so expectations need to be more humble.

Price and availability, in fact, are not decisive in judging the success or failure of interdiction. In the first place, no one who has argued for interdiction believes that it would stop all illegal drugs or stop efforts to produce and use them. In the face of two of the most powerful motives—the desire for altered states of consciousness and the desire to turn a profit—human nature and ingenuity will find a way no matter how serious the effort to stop them. Second, the real world of drug trafficking is a reactive one. Trafficking is big business, and traffickers are well-organized and well-financed. They can and do learn from their mistakes, and their size and diversification mean that they can survive even heavy blows aimed at their operations. Thus, for every action taken against them, they adjust and respond with new initiatives. Since interdiction alone cannot completely control trafficking or use, it cannot stop them. Its aim, however, is not a final solution, only a workable one.

Complete success is not a justifiable criterion for judging the success or failure of prohibition.

The principal contribution of interdiction is to raise the risks and costs of trafficking and in using drugs. The effects are reflected in the high street price of illegal drugs, a price that already takes law enforcement into consideration. Arguments such as those by Peter Reuter, a drug analyst with the RAND Corporation, to the effect that more interdiction raises the price of drugs only marginally and is therefore of little use, thus are largely irrelevant. High prices and the risk of prosecution deter potential users and discourage many frequent users. They are one of the reasons people quit before their casual use can become an addiction. By keeping prices high, interdiction and enforcement are elements of demand reduction. At home, interdiction thus is not a supply-reduction strategy but a demand-reduction program, and part of a coherent social message that drug use is wrong and punishable. And it has worked. According to John Walters, former deputy director of the White House Office of National Drug Control Policy, the Bush Administration's interdiction efforts resulted in a significant reduction in the availability of cocaine. This not only drove up the price of the drug, but also coincided with a decline in cocaine-related deaths and a 27 percent reduction in cocaine-related emergency room treatments.[12] Internationally, the purpose of interdiction is to create difficulties for the major criminal groups that traffic in and profit from illicit drugs. The disappearance of the Medellin Cartel illustrates that resolve and perseverance work.

Evidence indicates that it is law enforcement and criminal justice pressure that leads many addicts into treatment.

The two key influences on potential users, as reported by addicts and casual users, are the risks they perceive in trying to buy drugs and the ease with which they can do so. The higher the risk and greater the difficulty, the higher the deterrent value. To be sure, this equation seldom works for hardcore addicts, but casual users are discouraged by a riskier environment. Further, interdiction and law enforcement efforts are visible representations of a social judgment about drug use. Clear, unequivocal standards send a signal to potential users, especially the young, about acceptable behavior.

From 1985 until recently, visible interdiction and enforcement have contributed to steady declines in all categories of drug use except among hardcore addicts. The decisive criteria for success in counter-drug programs lie in measuring the rates of use and addiction and changes in public attitudes, not in counting the total number of seizures or the present street price of a given drug. Data collected by the National Household Survey on Drug Abuse show that casual or non-addictive use of cocaine was "dropping dramatically" when the Reagan and Bush Administrations were stepping up interdiction efforts. A rough estimate during the period 1985 through 1992 was an almost 80 percent decline in non-addictive users of cocaine, significantly reducing the overall demand for the drug.[13] Advocates of legalization or treatment-only recognize this pattern in relation to their own position when they note that the measure of their success will not be availability, price, the amount of drugs seized, the number of people incarcerated, or the number of patients in treatment, but changes in public attitudes and declines in users and addiction rates.

By these addiction rate standards, the record of prohibition is impressive. By 1992, after a decade of increased enforcement and treatment efforts, national surveys showed that teenage drug use was at the lowest levels in 20 years; monthly cocaine use had dropped 78 percent; close to half of cocaine production was being seized and major trafficking organizations had been disrupted or eliminated; negative attitudes towards drug use were predominant in high schools and the broader public; drug costs remained high; and using drugs was widely seen as a risky choice. Taken in the context of the epidemic proportions of drug use during the 1960s and 1970s, these were stunning gains.[14] Interdiction is not solely responsible for this success; it also cannot be singled out as a failed element. It was and must be a component in any coherent strategy aimed at reducing drug use.

International interdiction

But what of the claim that interdiction distorts U.S. foreign policy and puts democracy at risk in such places as Bolivia, Colombia, or Peru? The ultimate question is whether interdiction contributes to the security of U.S. citizens, not whether it responds to the concerns of other countries. When a threat emanates from a foreign source, U.S. policy makers are obligated to respond. For example, when Libyan-sponsored terrorists killed Americans in Europe, American policy makers did not focus on whether a strong response would destabilize Libya, but on whether it would secure American interests. In considering drug issues, Americans are perfectly within their rights to demand that countries which are the source of dangerous drugs coming to the United States control production and trafficking, especially when the drugs are illegal in these countries and by international agreement. American policy makers are, of course, properly concerned about preserving democracy overseas. The consideration is whether U.S. interdiction efforts are a threat to democracy in these countries and, if so, whether the threat is so great that it outweighs the value of international efforts to interdict dangerous drugs.

In this context, certain facts are relevant. First, democracy in Bolivia and Peru has been shaky on its own terms, aggravated by the mismanagement of local authorities, long before any U.S. interdiction efforts. Second, the power of the drug lords to corrupt local society, to use violence to intimidate local authorities on a massive scale, and to suborn the institutions of justice, is so extensive that the true threat to democracy lies in the existence and continued operation of these criminal organizations. Far from targeting foreign countries, U.S. interdiction efforts are designed to work with these countries to strengthen domestic institutions and to resist their subversion and intimidation by increasingly powerful criminal cartels.

Argument 3: Enforcement has failed. Critics of counter-drug policy are fond of pointing out that the U.S. prison population is the highest in the world and that, despite draconian drug laws and punitive enforcement, drug use continues and drugs are readily available. The costs of imprisonment are heavy, they add, and the money misspent on enforcement could be employed better elsewhere; moreover, the fact that enforcement efforts fall disproportionately on minorities suggests that the policy is inherently racist. A more humane and compassionate approach, they say, would focus on treatment.

This is presented as *prima facie* evidence for dramatically changing U.S. drug policy. The basic assumption: Government action to enforce laws, not individuals who use drugs or break the law, is the real problem. Hence, Professor Friedman argues that "Had drugs been decriminalized 17 years ago, 'crack' would never have been invented (it was invented because the high cost of illegal drugs made it profitable to provide a cheaper version) and there would be far fewer addicts."[15] This is a truly breathtaking assertion.

Critics of existing laws also seem to believe that there is some appropriate level of prison population in relation to the general population that can be used to measure the linkage between prison size and counter-drug policy. Such an argument, if used to justify a similar position on child abuse, would never be taken seriously. But critics actually seem to use it in this case largely because they are uncomfortable with enforcing the laws on drug use.

Just as the continued presence of drugs does not prove the failure of interdiction, simple prison numbers and the fact that drug use continues do not prove that enforcement has failed. Nor do the statistics constitute sufficient grounds for a major change in policy. After two decades of virtual legalization in the 1960s and 1970s, followed by less than a decade of renewed enforcement during a palpable decline in social cohesion that produced dramatic increases in drug abuse and criminal behavior, the appropriate level of arrest and incarceration is still not clear. In fact, there is no way to establish such an appropriate level, and none of the advocates of this argument has advanced a specific figure.

Drugs and prison

Nationwide figures for 1991 show roughly 14 million arrests of all sorts. The largest proportion (29 percent) were for alcohol-related offenses such as public drunkenness, driving under the influence, under-age drinking, and disorderly conduct. Direct drug-abuse violations accounted for only 7 percent of the total, although drugs figured in some arrests for property and violent crime as well. In 1991, the state, local, and federal prison population for all offenses was roughly 1.2 million, or 0.5 percent of the U.S. population.[16] Is this percentage too high or disproportionate? If so, compared with what? Of this 1.2 million, roughly 22 percent were imprisoned primarily for drug offenses; the remaining 78 percent were imprisoned for other crimes, although many of these inmates also may have used drugs.

There has been a large increase in the number of Americans in jail as a result of increasingly effective drug law enforcement. But, contrary to the contentions of some critics, the majority of these offenders are not simple drug users specifically targeted by an overzealous criminal justice system.[17] The greatest increases were not from among addicts, who generally received less attention and lighter sentences, but from among pushers, enforcers, and organized crime groups—as would be expected after a period of relatively lax law enforcement and an explosion in drug-related criminal activities. There also has been an increase in the overall prison population as the result of increases in violent and property crimes quite apart from drugs.

Advocates of legalization and treatment-only say that the number of inmates in jail on drug-related charges has grown sharply because of increased enforcement; the figure generally given is a doubling between 1979 and 1988.[18] This figure is used to illustrate the alleged harm caused by enforcement, supposedly proved by the fact that drugs remain available despite the arrests. The conclusion: end the harm done by arresting people.

The contention that legalization would not trigger large increases in use is based on optimism rather than evidence.

But this is not a logical conclusion. At the same time that cocaine use and arrests sharply increased, hospital admissions for overdose and drug-related emergencies increased seven times, and crack-related incidents increased fifteen-fold.[19] The number of cocaine-addicted newborns is estimated to be 2.5 percent of live births in the United States, or roughly 100,000 children a year who made no independent choice to use drugs.[20] Overall health care and collateral costs have soared. But there is no connection between these overdose statistics and the claim that drug law enforcement has failed. Nor do these facts themselves justify a significant redirection of public policy. In point of fact, as enforcement increased in the 1980s there were dramatic declines in *overall* drug use. There is at least some evidence, then, as reflected in use and health care statistics, to suggest that law enforcement can reduce drug use and addiction rates.[21] There is no evidence to suggest that ending drug law enforcement efforts will lower use rates or the harm done by addiction. In fact, evidence indicates that it is law enforcement and criminal justice pressure that leads many addicts into treatment who would otherwise not seek help.

Still, advocates of a serious enforcement policy never claim that it would end drug use. The aim is to protect the public from the worst predators, engage in a struggle to reverse the trend of increasing drug use throughout the population, and send an unambiguous signal to potential new users that drug use has negative social consequences. Unlike hardliners who claim that a treatment-focused policy will produce a drug-free America, enforcement officials recognize that enforcement—like interdiction—is only one instrument in a range of policies that must be employed. Even then, human nature being what it is, no combination of policies will end drug use. Any claim that offers a magic bullet is classic oversell that demands the best possible result in advance.

Critics of enforcement policies go on to claim that the money spent on enforcement and prisons is disproportionately high and should be spent on treatment which would end drug use and crime. One would expect such claims to be based on strong evidence, but the numbers thrown about do not demonstrate either that there is a causal connection or even a correlation between money spent on treatment and reductions in crime or drugs, or that money spent on prisons is wasted. No such connection is demonstrable. No count of prisoners, no budget totals, no indicator of current and heavy use of drugs has established that enforcement money is misspent or that treatment instead of enforcement is a better cure. The question in any case requires an answer based on social values and a public consensus, not on data alone, and the American people have answered that they consider enforcement essential to any solution.

Consider also the claim that enforcement is unfair and racist.[22] What is the evidence? Simply that more minorities, particularly black Americans, than other groups are in prison for drug-related offenses as a proportion of the population. For those who use such numbers to justify race-norming, this argument makes sense, but it is wide of the mark.[23] In fact, most black offenders are in jail for black-on-black crimes. That a larger proportion of blacks is in prison is explained by the uncomfortable fact that street crime is more prevalent in primarily black, inner-city neighborhoods than elsewhere and that it occurs more openly and therefore is more easily solved and prosecuted. The alternative to enforcement is to leave the decent citizens in inner-city black neighborhoods—the vast majority—to fend for themselves among the predators.

Consider that data on regular cocaine use from the National Institute on Drug Abuse (NIDA) show that twice as many men as women use cocaine but that drug arrests run five men for every one woman because men are more likely than women to commit violent crimes and are therefore more subject to arrest. These figures are not said to establish discrimination against men or in favor of women. Moreover, in cities with black mayors and chiefs of police, the proportions of arrests among whites and blacks are the same as for the rest of the country. Unless one assumes that even in these cases racism is the only explanation for different arrest rates, the argument does not hold. Using raw figures on arrests and simple comparisons of percentages to draw self-serving conclusions is a familiar, but invalid, practice.[24]

The dangers of drug use

Argument 4: Drug use is not that bad. Some advocates of legalization contend that the dangers of drug use are overstated and do not warrant strong enforcement efforts. Taken literally, this argument was more plausible in the 1960s and 1970s, when less was known about the full effects of many drugs. Few now claim that the use of psychotropic drugs represents no serious health hazard and that use should be celebrated as a liberation of consciousness. Instead, the most visible spokesmen for this view, such as Professor Ethan Nadelmann of the Woodrow Wilson School, assert that such drug use represents no special liability, certainly none greater than tobacco or alcohol, that justifies prohibition.[25] "The logic of legalization," says Nadelmann, "depends in part upon two assumptions: that most illegal drugs are not as dangerous as is commonly believed, and that the most risky of them are unlikely to prove widely appealing precisely because of the obvious danger."[26]

This is not an isolated view. Steven Duke and Albert Gross, in their book *America's Longest War: Rethinking Our Tragic Crusade Against Drugs,* with an introduction by Baltimore mayor Kurt Schmoke, offer the observation that "The risks of psychoactive drug use are substantial but no greater than those accompanying many other recreational activities" such as hang-gliding, boxing, mountain climbing, motorcycle riding, hunting, bicycle riding, or boating.[27] Echoing Nadelmann, they argue that "the use of heroin and cocaine in a free market system would adversely affect the quality of the lives of the users and those around them in a way not appreciably different than does alcohol use" and that "the total number of drug abusers . . . would not be essentially different than is the case in our hybrid system of legalization."[28] Or, "Hardly anyone would be a drug abuser who does not already abuse at least one psychoactive drug."

For this to be true, for the same number of people engaged in these other "risky" activities as in using drugs, one would expect to see a corresponding number of lives cut short and other consequences. Thus, one would have to expect that some loss of life, increased health care costs, lost labor, family violence, higher crime, damaged fetuses, and so forth be counted among the costs of recreational biking, boxing, hunting, sports, gardening, and similarly risky behaviors. For example, drug-using workers are 3 to 4 times as likely to have on-the-job accidents, 4 to 6 times more likely to have off-the-job accidents, 2 to 3 times more likely to file medical claims, 5 times more likely to file workman's compensation, and 25 percent to 35 percent less productive on the job.[29] Yet nobody suggests that bicycling addicts and others impose corresponding broad-ranging increases in personal costs that the whole community must bear.

Americans are not living in the 1970s, or the age of *Reefer Madness*, when there was little scientific research on the addictive nature of psychotropic drugs or the considerable health consequences of prolonged exposure to them. Quite the contrary. Recent medical evidence on the effects of drug use has forced supporters of legalization to stress the need for sustained, vigorous treatment programs—a frank admission that there is a serious health hazard. But they still downplay the dangerous aspects of drug use. Even if this hazard were no greater than that represented by tobacco (a generous concession) there would be no comfort in recapitulating the catastrophe of widespread tobacco use.

Tobacco is implicated directly in some 300,000 premature deaths in the United States each year. The immense collateral costs in health care requirements, lost labor, damaged fetuses, and debilitated lives run to billions of dollars. Reliable figures place drug-related premature deaths, at current levels of use, at somewhere between 3,000 and 20,000,[30] added to which are the correspondingly high collateral costs. An intuitive argument would hold that as psychotropic drug use increased after legalization, the death toll and collateral costs also would rise. Legalization arguments ignore this. But what of the second assumption: that legalization would not result in dramatic increases in the use of these drugs precisely because they are so dangerous?

International experience

The contention that legalization would not trigger large increases in use is based on optimism rather than evidence. Of course, the contention cannot be proved without a state or nationwide experiment in legalization. Americans are encouraged to accept it as an article of faith. There is, however, international evidence that argues for the opposite conclusion. In 1987, Zurich, Switzerland, opened Platzspitz Park as a haven for heroin addicts. The idea was based on tolerance. Initially, there were only a handful of addicts, but word quickly spread among Europe's growing heroin-addicted population that Platzspitz Park was a haven for drug users. The park quickly became a disaster area. Addicts poured in, but more important, local addiction soared. And the park itself became a dangerous place. Ultimately, reacting to public outrage, city officials reversed themselves and ended the experiment.[31]

The Netherlands offers another example. Often hailed as the best model of social tolerance of drug use, the Netherlands has chosen largely not to enforce anti-drug laws and to tolerate drug use in specific areas, particularly certain sections of Amsterdam. The assumption was that tolerance and a good treatment program would deal with the addict population, which would gradually wither away when users understood the inherent dangers of drug use, and that drug use and again the crime associated with it would remain isolated. Instead, as in Platzspitz Park, addicts from all over Europe came to the Netherlands, and the local addict population has soared. Crime also has soared, both in the specified areas and more generally. Today, by some estimates, the Netherlands is the most crime-prone nation in Europe, and authorities are reconsidering many of their basic assumptions in the face of public pressure. Furthermore, Dutch efforts to license legal heroin use quickly ran aground amid huge increases in crime and overdose deaths, despite generous treatment and information programs.[32] As one advocate of legalization admits, "We have a lot to learn from the Dutch."[33]

None of the claims made by legalization advocates . . . justify so vast a social experiment.

Historical evidence in the United States also suggests that drug use would soar if drugs were legalized. Americans can examine the vast social experiment with drugs in the 1960s and 1970s. Liberal political leaders, the popular press, Hollywood, intellectuals, and other "opinion makers" downplayed the dangers of drug use, when they did not extol it, and pushed for nonenforcement of existing anti-drug laws. It was a pervasive social message: Drug use is a personal choice with no serious negative side effects or socially deleterious consequences. While not everyone went as far as Dr. Timothy Leary in celebrating the new age of a higher humanity thanks to LSD, the cumulative message was unmistakable. America's youth got the point. There was an explosion in use—despite widespread information on the negative health implications—followed by a crime wave, increased social violence, and growing health care costs. Drug traffickers also got the message, profiting handsomely.

Prohibition did not create this increase in crime and social problems. *De facto* legalization did. But according to legalization advocates, the reaction to the problem of drug addiction from the 1960s and 1970s was overblown by hysterical researchers, moralizing do-gooders, conservative politicians, and the mindless press; the health care costs of illegal drugs also allegedly were exaggerated. In short, the problem did not justify all the fuss.[34] And based on the assumption that the present user population would not increase with legalization, they claim that future costs will not be as bad as projected, and will not be as bad as for tobacco or alcohol—

or at least will be no worse if drugs are legalized.

Needless to say, these views are subject to challenge. There is nothing to justify a claim that the drug epidemic was the figment of narrow-minded moralizers, that it was not all that serious, and that the costs were exaggerated. The facts point to a very different conclusion. And there is nothing in the available evidence to show that society should not hold drug users to a measure of responsibility for their acts or continue to control access to dangerous drugs.

Argument 5: We permit the use of tobacco and alcohol; why not drugs? Proponents of legalization argue that illegal drugs should be treated the same as tobacco and alcohol. This is another argument by analogy. Tobacco and alcohol are legal, and yet they are responsible for 500,000 premature deaths a year and staggering health care and allied costs. Therefore, because psychotropic drugs kill far fewer people at present levels of use—which supposedly will not increase—America should legalize them and treat the insignificant consequences that follow.

Proponents of this argument use a barrage of facts to show the sad consequences of legalized tobacco and alcohol, arguing that because tobacco and alcohol are legal and cause collateral damage, America should legalize psychoactive drugs. Not only is this illogical, it establishes no causal relationship between the elements. Indeed, the reverse can be argued: Prohibit the use of tobacco and alcohol because of the immense harm they do. Such a prohibition is not politically feasible in the case of tobacco, but it certainly is more logical than saying that because alcohol and tobacco take a terrible toll, a heavy toll from legalizing drugs is therefore acceptable.

One can imagine the storm of ridicule that would accompany a suggestion that business should be permitted to increase the production of environmentally unsafe wastes because firms already produce so much, or that enforcement of environmental laws should be made merely symbolic because so much damage has already been done. Such an argument could not be made seriously in public. Yet advocates of legalization seem to enjoy a certain cachet, especially among elite audiences, when they use the same brand of logic. If anything, the considerable social and economic costs of dealing with the legal use of tobacco and alcohol are substantive arguments for not adding to the collective woe by legalizing dangerous drugs.

Treatment for drug abuse

Argument 6: The only rational policy is a treatment approach. Treatment figures prominently in the legalization argument. To legalization advocates, drug abuse is no more than a medical problem needing treatment; any other approach is misplaced, bound to fail, and wasteful. From this position, they claim that treatment linked to education about the risks of drug abuse is the only strategy needed to deal with any residual problems from drug use following legalization; this treatment-only approach, in conjunction with legalization, will end drug abuse, reduce crime, and deter future abuse, or at least keep it at an acceptable level. They dismiss the notion that cheap, readily available legal drugs will mean a significant increase in use, apparently not even believing that manufacturers of legalized drugs would find inventive ways to advertise their products to increase sales. They consider that money spent on anything other than treatment programs is wasted.

To be fair, not everyone who favors a treatment strategy wants to legalize, or dismisses complementary control efforts so completely. Mathea Falco, to her credit, rejects the idea. She favors significant redirection of funds from law enforcement to treatment, which she expects to end addiction and deter future use. Her concept of demand-control strategy, however, basically undercuts the efficacy of any other approach, taking away with one hand what it seems to give with the other. Most treatment professionals, doctors, and many public health officials also are not for legalization. Their main concern is with the quality of present treatment, which many believe is poor and inadequate. They tend to believe that there is too much focus on enforcement, and many of their claims for treatment are hyperbole designed to attract attention and force a reallocation of public money to them in line with their priorities. To be sure, this is indeed a budget battle over who gets how much for what purpose. But advocates have yet to provide evidence that spending, say, 80 percent on treatment and 20 percent on enforcement will produce all the wonders claimed for such a shift.

Unfortunately, many treatment-only advocates endorse the encompassing view of the benefits to be anticipated from legalization and therapeutic-only policies generally. For this reason, there is little practical difference between them and proponents of outright legalization. Treatment-only advocates do not object to drug use; they merely assert that demand reduction based on treatment is the only practical way to reduce or end the drug abuse problem. Use is permissible, abuse is a medical problem, and both will wither away before beneficent, compassionate therapy. It is this view that attracts most of the attention and distorts discussion of a serious national problem.

This position is a defining characteristic of today's legalization argument: Treatment is the only workable and realistic answer to drug abuse. All others are futile or worse. Adopt this approach and "The world would be healthier, safer, and more humane."[35]

In its distilled form, a treatment-only focus implicitly means that treatment will deter future use and that treatment and education will do what no other policy has done or can do—create a drug-free America.[36] According to this view, if it is known that treatment for drug abuse is available, linked to tobacco-type awareness programs, it will be possible to persuade the young and other potentially vulnerable populations not adept at recognizing the negative long-term consequences of immediately pleasing choices to refrain from using drugs. The inescapable conclusion is that people will choose to be drug-free. "Repeal of drug prohibition respects the decision-making ability of each individual," writes Kevin Zeese. "The individual is responsible for his or her own health and well-being rather than the government. When presented with the true risks of drug use most individuals will make sensible choices."[37]

Most legalization or treatment-only advocates do not claim that 100 percent success is possible, but all seem to believe that prohibition and enforcement have failed and cannot work because they have not had 100 percent success. Treatment is said to be the best approach because of its inherent promise to make America a drug-free society, although one searches in vain for any evidence for such a bold contention. What is often offered as evidence is either the British experience with heroin control (or that of the Netherlands) or the U.S. experience with reducing tobacco use. Because these worked, it is argued, drug treatment in a legalized environment will work.

The British experience

In essence, the British in the 1920s and for 40 years thereafter had a largely treatment-only philosophy for dealing with heroin addiction.[38] The government did not legalize heroin, but created a treatment regime where existing, known addicts were given access to medical care and supervision. Initially, this also meant that doctors could prescribe controlled heroin doses to their addicted patients, most of whom were women and middle-class. This was a policy based on the idea of heroin use as an illness; it seemed to be humane, healthy, and compassionate.

By the 1980s, the system was in ruins. There was a sudden explosion in heroin use, generally linked to the huge increase in worldwide supply. By the mid-1980s, with the official blind eye to heroin use, known addiction rates were increasing at about 30 percent per year, but indications were that actual use was 5 or 20 times that of officially acknowledged levels.[39] In 1960, there were just 68 heroin addicts known to the British government. In 1968, there were 2,000. But by 1982, there were 20,000 in London alone.[40] Addicts no longer were mostly women or middle-class, but came from every part of society. Doctors learned that prescribing set doses of heroin did not satisfy their patients' demand for drugs, which grew with use. The therapeutic question became whether to continue to supply the drug at unsafe levels, contrary to medical ethics, or to resist, which meant patients would buy heroin on the streets. Doctors also discovered that some patients sold their legal supplies to others. Doctors then shifted to prescribing methadone. Addiction to heroin still soared. There was a nationwide education campaign on the dangers of heroin, but addiction soared even higher. The British public demanded action. The government pursued a mixed policy of supply control and demand control, but addiction still rose. It continues to rise, compounded by growing cocaine addiction and rising crime.

The question becomes: If complete success is the criterion for adopting an approach, what happens when neither demand nor supply control works? One could simply do nothing, but nothing means letting addiction find its natural level (whatever that is), hoping that legal drugs will not lead to increased use and even higher health and other social costs. The British treatment approach did not end or reduce addiction; nor did the British save a great deal of money. If the criterion for adopting a program is that it will succeed where others have failed, the British example does not even come close to making the case for treatment only.

The tobacco experience

Tobacco use is another area "treatment advocates" cite to show what is possible. In the last 25 years, over half of all cigarette users have given up smoking, not because cigarettes were illegal or users faced imprisonment, but because of highly successful public information programs and social pressure to quit. This experience is cited as a model for how we should deal with drugs: legalize them and convince Americans not to use them.

The tobacco experience, however, is not necessarily a good model for drug legalizers. Today, after an immense effort, including heavy moralizing and growing restrictions on smoking, there are still 55 million smokers and 300,000 tobacco-related premature deaths a year. Costs of tobacco-related heath care run at about $60 billion each year. By comparison, annual enforcement, current health care, and collateral costs for illegal drugs run between $40 billion and $50 billion; imprisonment costs for all 1.2 million inmates run about $16 billion.[41] If America maintains this level of efficiency in reducing tobacco use for another 25 years, there will be only 25 million smokers, 150,000 deaths, and (with inflation) another $60 billion in costs. From this chain of logic, one is supposed to conclude that success with tobacco will be repeated with psychotropic drugs after legalization. But is this progress with tobacco compelling reason to legalize drugs? Even if one were to make the unwarranted assumption that there will be no substantial increase in the number of drug users from present levels after legalization, one would still have to accept at least 10,000 or so deaths and, conservatively, $50 billion in health care and related costs each year. Moreover, if there is an increase in use and addiction, these costs will rise. That "if" is critical.

Legalization and treatment advocates employ a sleight-of-hand, however, to suggest there will be no increases in drug use. Although they denigrate the war on drugs as a total failure, many nonetheless acknowledge that overall use has declined from the previous high levels of the 1970s and 1980s. They attribute this to demand-reduction efforts, especially to greater public awareness of the dangers of drugs, but seem to suggest that this awareness arose spontaneously. Why?

The spontaneous awareness view assumes that vigorous enforcement and supply-control efforts made no contribution to public awareness that drugs were bad. Instead, society somehow just came to its senses. Moreover, according to this line of reasoning, this heightened awareness will contain future demand, even if the government changes its position to suggest that drug use is acceptable. Advocates of legalization confidently expect, for example, that since only a small percentage of the 20 million or so who tried cocaine when it was illegal became frequent users, legalizing cocaine use would lead to no increase in addiction. To ordinary Americans, this may sound like nonsense, but this is the inherent logic of the treatment-only and legalization arguments.

A personal choice?

Argument 7: It is no business of government. A common position of legalization advocates is that drug use is a matter of personal choice and therefore should be beyond government regulation. To many Americans who resent government regulation, this is the most persuasive of all the arguments for legalization.

The American democratic republic is premised on the rights of the citizen against the government and the insistence that government not be permitted to transgress these rights, among which is a limit on government interference in the private interests and personal choices of individuals. At a time when the federal government is inventing more reasons to intrude into every aspect of Americans' personal lives, this is a vital concern.

Drug use, the argument thus runs, is a personal choice. It affects no one but the user. No harm is caused to others, so government has no right to interfere, even if intervention might benefit the individual. By logical extension, this would mean that if the individual became an addict who needed treatment, the rest of society, acting through the government, would have no legal or moral obligation to respond, although few legalization advocates are quite so rigorous in pursuing the argument to such a conclusion.

The most persuasive argument for this harm-minimization approach is found in John Stuart Mill's classic work of political theory, *On Liberty*. Mill argues that the coercive powers of the state should not be used against an individual unless that person is engaged in acts harmful to others. Individuals must have a significant range of choice over the decisions that affect their lives, and the state should not interfere with the free exercise of that wide-ranging liberty. This "self-regarding" or "self-determining" philosophy seeks to maximize the individual's freedom of choice: "the sole end for which mankind are warranted, individually or collectively," in Mill's formulation,

> in interfering with the liberty of action of any of their number, is self protection . . . the only purpose for which power can be rightfully exercised over any member of a civilized community, against his will, is to prevent harm to others. His own good, either physical or moral, is not sufficient warrant, he cannot rightfully be compelled to do or forbear because it would be better for him to do so, because it will make him happier, because, in the opinion of others to do so would be wise or even right.[42]

This noble argument rightly recognizes the necessity of balancing individual rights and responsibilities and the authority of the state. But Mill himself recognized that individuals and their rights do not exist in a vacuum, and accepted that individual rights also carry with them an individual responsibility to others not to act in a way that will cause harm. Rights, in other words, have reciprocal obligations.

Advocates present the case for legalization as if, by definition, drug use cannot harm others, so there is no reciprocal obligation to refrain from use. They argue further that the only harm derives from the effort to restrict this free choice or, on balance, that the harm of enforcing a prohibition is far worse than any harm caused by personal use. Thus, all efforts by society to restrain individual access to drugs, to control use, and to punish breaches of the law are immoral because they are unjustified.

In this light, the six arguments already discussed here, despite their logical inconsistencies and factual shortcomings, begin to make sense. It becomes clearer why the claims are made that drugs themselves are not so harmful, that legalization will mean no costly increases in addicts, why prisons will empty and streets will become safe, and why Americans can expect nothing but savings from legal, taxable drugs. It is important for legalizers to make these claims, because once one acknowledges the possibility that harm might be done to others by a personal choice to use drugs, the entire personal-rights position becomes untenable.

The problem is that harm is done. Many graphic examples exist to demonstrate the social harm caused by this individual choice (Figures on crime and HIV exposure are not included here because it might be argued—and often is—that these problems are the result of prohibition and enforcement).

Some 25 percent to 60 percent of the homeless are addicts whose homelessness is due in large part to addiction and their inability to manage money or make rational, reasonable decisions. They are increasingly supported at public expense because of the moral obligation felt by society. The harm is done not only to themselves, therefore, but also to the taxpayers and others in society who feel obligated to help the homeless.

Some 75 percent to 80 percent of the 1.2 million to 1.5 million teenage runaways are substance abusers, and not because prohibition made them use drugs or run away. The harm is done not only to themselves, but also to their parents and those who have to deal with the consequences.

Some 30 percent to 50 percent of mental patients are chemical abusers, and 50 percent to 60 percent of these are users of crack and cocaine. They are largely on public support. The harm is done to the taxpayers.

The logic of legalization is fundamentally flawed.

As many as 11 percent of young mothers use drugs during pregnancy. The harm is not just to these young mothers, but to their unborn children. Approximately 2.5 percent of all live births—some 100,000 babies per year—are born addicted to cocaine. They have life-long learning disabilities and emotional problems. Once again, the harm is done to unborn children and to taxpayers who must pay the treatment bills. And the harm can last a lifetime.

About $50 billion is devoted annually to dealing with the health care and other collateral costs of drug addiction. These would not disappear with legalization and almost certainly would increase. This harm is done to anyone who has to pay higher private insurance premiums or higher taxes for public health programs, to pay these costs incurred by addicts.

There are approximately 500,000 heroin and 2 million other substance abusers. Their care is increasingly a demand on society. Once again, the harm is done to the taxpayer.

Legalization advocates tend to respond to these numbers by countering that the costs of enforcement and prohibition are greater and therefore somehow cancel out these costs. As an example, they argue that incarceration costs, which run about $16 billion a year for all offenders, of whom some 22 percent are in jail for drug crimes, are so disproportionate as to obviate any theoretical harm from personal drug use. The problems of addicted babies are the result of poverty and social conditions, not drugs; and so on.

The bargain-basement mentality of legalization advocates includes this interesting bit of arithmetic: legal drugs will return immense revenues from taxes, which will more than cover the diminishing costs of treatment and related drug problems. It is hardly likely that anyone would accept this notion if applied to alcohol and tobacco, in addition to which legalization advocates seem to assume that the taxable profits from legal drugs will be on a par with profits from illegal drugs—which are some 9 times higher than a legal price is likely to be—in a population that is not going to use the drugs anyway. If that were the case, taxes on legal drugs would not even come close to paying for the medical and treatment costs of a fraction of the treatment population unless the taxes were so high as to make bootlegging attractive, which defeats the purpose of legalizing.

Moral consequences

Since advocates of legalization invoke the language and logic of morals in order to defend their position, it might also be appropriate to raise, as part of the harm done, the moral consequences for others from this personal choice. What is at issue is whether the community has a right to interfere in personal choices to protect community interests. Most Americans recognize that "We have laws . . . precisely because we cannot leave the vindication or avoidance of wrongs to the commands of self-interest. When our obligations collide with our 'interests,' even men and women with the best of intentions may need an additional support to firm them up in their strength to choose what is right and avoid what is wrong."[43] To the extent that even the most ardent legalization advocates—apart from the Leary wing of the movement—recognize the harm done to individuals by drugs, they acknowledge a public interest. In particular, they recognize that drug addiction deprives individuals of many of the attributes of individuality: the ability to exercise free judgment, to recognize responsibility, and to render respect to others. As James Q.Wilson notes, "Nicotine alters one's habits, cocaine alters one's soul." Wilson continues,

> The heavy use of crack, unlike the heavy use of tobacco, corrodes those natural sentiments of sympathy and duty that constitute our human nature and make possible our social life. To say, as does Nadelmann, that distinguishing morally between tobacco and cocaine is "little more than a transient prejudice" is close to saying that morality itself is but a prejudice.[44]

Since Nadelmann himself invokes the language of morality to argue against prohibition, he must accept that morality is more than a prejudice; if not, his position carries no weight.

If there is no common standard to which we may appeal in such matters of public concern, then virtually any putatively consensual act is permissible. Sex with a consenting minor, for example, is no more morally offensive than ignoring a sign prohibiting walking on a lawn. Yet there are no advocates of drug legalization or harm minimization—who abhor the thought of someone else's idea of morality being enforced on others—who would favor permitting someone to molest children. The harm-minimization advocate would respond that molestation harms the child and thus violates an innocent who is not fully competent to make a truly independent choice. But this argument invokes two criteria—the need to demonstrate harm done to another and the need to show that the other was not competent to choose. These criteria mirror exactly the fundamental questions at issue with respect to drug abuse: does the drug abuser harm anyone else, and is the addict competent to choose whether or not to continue use?

The problem is that those who favor drug legalization or harm minimization dismiss both arguments as irrelevant when it suits their case and invoke them again when it suits. By arguing that drug users should be treated rather than left strictly free to continue using drugs, however, legalization advocates admit that the community must act to prevent or limit harm to users. Such action imposes a cost on the community. The very claim that treatment, in some cases even mandatory treatment, is the answer to drug abuse is an admission that harm is done beyond individual choice. This harm is done to the community that must pay for treatment, to the family affected by a drug-abusing member, to the work force that must risk drug-impaired workers, to babies who are truly innocent victims. Furthermore, drug use leading to addiction, which is a profound risk for anyone using psychoactive drugs, also leads to a loss of volition, of the competence necessary to make a truly informed, independent choice. No one decides to use drugs because he wants to become an addict. No one thinks it will happen to him. It happens nevertheless.

If one accepts the legalization interpretation of the harm-minimization argument, one is left with this anomaly: Surely we must accord the individual the right to be an addict; but, recognizing the consequences of addiction, the user has no corresponding obligation to avoid use, and society no right to make him do so.

Most important of all, Congress must not legalize drugs.

The harm-minimization argument thus falls short on the very issue of self-determination upon which it is based. The exercise of liberty depends upon the ability to exercise self-determination. The irony is that drug abuse, while it may have begun as a volitional act, ends in the loss of volition to the demands of an addiction. The defining characteristic of the self-determining individual is lost. Since it can be known in advance that this will be the likely outcome of drug use, it is cruel indeed to argue that it is an individual's sacred right to destroy the very faculties that define him as a person and society's duty to assist him, and knowing this, it is a strange and malicious charity that would have society help someone to acquire an addiction rather than take steps to prevent it if possible.

Underlying the "freedom" argument also seems to be the notion that the individual bears no responsibility for personal choice and that, somehow, addiction is society's fault and the victim is owed reparations. This same claim is advanced in other areas of American social life. Not long ago, Americans routinely spoke of the criminal paying his debt to society; now liberal academics speak of society being to blame for creating the conditions leading to criminal behavior. But the problem of drug addiction is the result not of some decisions by a rational entity called "society," but of individual choices that create a social concern. Until policy makers clearly understand this, they are bound to have difficulty sorting out the proper relationships between individual rights and limits on government authority. If human beings, as Aristotle noted, were beasts or gods, no law would be necessary; there would be no need to intervene in their personal choices. This not being the case, human society is built on law and the obligations of each in relation to all. Faced with the question of drugs, society retains a right and a duty to act, even if the chances of success are considerably less than 100 percent.

What kind of legalization might policy makers adopt?

Even if federal or state policy makers were persuaded by these seven spurious arguments in favor of legalization, they would have to decide what form of legalization to introduce. What version promises safer drugs, removal of profit to criminals, safer streets, fewer addicts, fewer criminals, better civil rights, humane policies, deglamorized drugs, and even new tax revenues? Options range from complete legalization of all drugs for all people to controlled legalization that would limit the drugs available and who can buy them. There is no consensus among legalization advocates, some of whom say the issue needs more study, but a representative list of approaches typically includes the following:

- Legalize heroin, cocaine, and marijuana outright (or perhaps in phases), but set an appropriate minimum age, such as now applies to alcohol, for buyers. As a variation, legalize possession but not selling (ironically, the equivalent of alcohol prohibition in the 1930s). Permit only licensed clinics to dispense the more dangerous heroin and cocaine as a prescription drug (as in the British example) while offering treatment to users.
- Continue to restrict more dangerous "designer" drugs. Many legalization advocates recognize the logical inconsistency of arguing for restraints on some drugs but not all; even some of the more ardent recognize that enterprising chemists might produce truly frightening concoctions.
- Prohibit advertising for the sale of these items as part of the effort to keep people from buying them.
- Substantially increase funding for research to find a safe substitute for existing drugs, to develop safer forms of these drugs, or to determine just how dangerous or safe particular drugs are.
- Vastly increase funding of treatment and prevention programs—supposedly to be paid for with the savings from law enforcement and tax revenues from drugs that have been legalized.
- End virtually all drug testing except in jobs affecting safety, such as airline pilots.
- Stop all the negative rhetoric about the "War on Drugs" and wage peace instead.

These approaches will work, advocates claim, because "America is becoming more health conscious. . . . Drugs will not stand in the way of this fitness revolution. The citizenry knows better."[45] They will work because it is wrong to interfere in people's personal choices, because they will take the profit motive out of crime, because they will end urban blight, punitive moralizing, and perhaps even tooth decay. They will lead to fewer addicts or, at worst, to people who know how to use drugs more rationally and moderately.

One can raise objections to all of these options, and many have been discussed in this analysis, but one or two additional observations might be useful. Legalization advocates recognize that society has a right and an obligation to control access to dangerous substances that might harm individuals and others. This is the basis for placing an age limit on use. No one wants minors to have access to drugs. But, what is a minor? The age limit is variable. To a legalizer, it is probably around eighteen. To a seller, it is probably around seven, because a seven-year-old has lunch money and an allowance. In any event, it is generally accepted that there should be laws to prevent the sale of drugs to minors, but how does this avoid the very objections to prohibition that legalization advocates raise? Advocates seem to assume that enforcement in this case will not lead to the "forbidden fruit" mentality or produce more crime and addiction because minors will know they are not competent to make personal choices open to adults. Further, they naively believe that producers and marketers of drugs will accept these age limits and that criminal organizations will not try to addict younger Americans.

Some legalization advocates also maintain that America can legalize some dangerous drugs and not others, but what is the logical basis for doing so? How does one avoid violating the rights of users and creating the same prohibition-driven suite of crimes and misdemeanors that are condemned now as so inherently wrong? Having essentially scrapped enforcement and the rationale for it, how does one combat the organized crime groups that will exploit this market? If an enforcement capability for such prohibited drugs is retained, how much is society justified in spending on it? Some legalization advocates suggest a 90/10 split—that is, 90 percent to treatment and prevention, and 10 percent to enforcement. A moment's reflection, however, will show that there is no rational basis for such a split. So policy makers are back to the same troubling public policy question of how to determine the amount of time and money that is needed and who among the many claimants will get the resources.

Even most legalization advocates recognize the harm that drugs do and propose ways to lessen their effects.

It would be possible to continue piling up the logical inconsistencies, the conclusions based on desires, and the expectations based on hope. The point, however, should be clear: None of the claims made by legalization advocates, in and of themselves, meet the test of factual certainty or logical necessity that would justify so vast a social experiment. There is nothing in the logic of these claims that overrides the expressed public conviction that legalization is wrong.

Legalization's advocates make expansive claims for their solution. Admittedly, all public policy debates require a degree of hyperbole to overcome social inertia (certainly, advocates of the War on Drugs have committed sins in this regard), and supposed cure-alls are not uncommon in political discourse. Drama aside, however, what is appropriate in public posturing is not appropriate in trying to reach a sober assessment of what to do. In the case of drug control, the evidentiary standards for dramatic shifts in public policy that override experience demand more than posturing and confident assurances.

If there is no such conclusive evidence for a substantive shift, the inherent logic of the position must be conclusive and convincing. But the logic of legalization is fundamentally flawed. Legalization claims as its outcome an end to drug-related crime, a drop in drug use, an increase in public awareness of the dangers of drug use, a corresponding decline in all collateral costs, a deterrent to any increased use, and an end to the need for draconian state intervention in private lives—in short, a panacea.

It is no wonder that, at first blush, the argument is so appealing. It is categorical and untroubled by the contingent outcomes that so bedevil other, less self-confident claims. As the previous analysis indicates, however, legalization cannot deliver on any of these promises.

Why America needs a more consistent drug policy

America has not been served very well by the rhetoric of the War on Drugs. Whatever short-term advantages it may have offered as a public relations tool to win support for a difficult, long-term effort, in the end it was a rhetorical bonanza for legalization's advocates and sympathizers. It has become muddled with the imagery of a war, with metaphors of timely, unconditional victory, of an honorable peace, and of a return to normalcy. This rhetoric is misleading and has led to many of the charges raised against the campaign—that it cannot succeed, that it is futile, and that enforcement has not stopped trafficking and use, lowered the price, or reduced availability. If it cannot be won, they proceed, why spend the time and money? Wars end. This one has not. Society cannot win, so declare peace.

But there can be no "peace." If America cannot end drug production and use, and yet cannot give in to the temptation to give up, what are the options? The problems of drug use are not simple and will not respond to simple solutions. It must be understood that there can be no victory parade, at least not in the sense of ending the problem, only manageable limits.

The Reagan and Bush Administrations were on the right track, and their strategy was the product of 25 years of trial and error, of public frustration and congressional pressure. In essence, it codified a lesson-learning process. The lesson is simple: America needs to engage; it needs money; it needs the President on board; it needs to demand interagency coordination; it needs to coordinate law enforcement efforts with intelligence and military efforts; it needs to involve the international community; it must have a strategy that relies on both demand- and supply-reduction approaches; it needs patience, stamina, and perseverance—even a sense of humor.

The difficulty for policy makers lies in figuring out how all these parts interrelate to produce something that has some coherence. Policy makers

must balance conflicting claims, resolve maddening "turf" issues, and develop budget priorities, which means striking a balance between resources spent on demand reduction efforts and those spent on supply. As part of this, however, it is important not to set them up as opposite poles but to realize that they are complementary. The Bush Administration placed more emphasis on supply reduction because that was the area longest neglected and the one in which the public saw the most immediate threat. It nevertheless also substantially increased demand-reduction programs. Supply reduction and enforcement efforts, in fact, are part of any sophisticated demand-reduction program; conversely, reducing demand will influence supply and price.

America also needs indicators of success. As suggested earlier, these lie in public perceptions of the appropriateness of drug use, in attitudes toward use and perceptions of risk (including punishment), and in learning whether use is growing. For many of the measures employed in responding to this threat, little direct pay-off will ever be seen. Enforcement, for example, is not a solution, but only one instrument in a comprehensive effort. It keeps prices high, adds weight to the social message that drugs are bad, makes life more difficult for criminals, and helps keep drugs away from most people. In isolation, however, it does not deter drug use.

More specifically, policy makers need to

- Construct more prisons and improve existing ones.
- Enforce tougher laws for distribution and sale of illegal drugs.
- Expand education efforts.
- Increase funding for community-based programs of treatment, education, and enforcement.
- Increase funding for drug research.
- Increase funding for treatment and conduct a careful review of existing programs for effectiveness as a justification for funding.
- Make greater efforts to engage international cooperation on law enforcement, interdiction, extradition, financial crimes, and eradication, linking development assistance to progress on drug control.

Finally, policy makers must recognize the long-haul nature of the problem and eschew quick-fix metaphors. Americans need to be told that we are in a reactive environment in which someone is waiting to respond to whatever is done. Policy makers must keep explaining their policy to the public.

Most important of all, Congress must not legalize drugs.

Drugs will never be eliminated

Americans can never reasonably expect to eliminate drug production and use. Declaring war on murder will not end it, and there will be no end to the struggle against drug use. But neither is it possible to accept drug use as an inevitable evil. To do so would cause social chaos. Even most legalization advocates recognize the harm that drugs do and propose ways to lessen their effects. The difference is that they believe individual claims override community ones, that the evil of drug use is preferable to worse evil of oppressive and intrusive government, but their evidence is not compelling and their logic, even less so.

After seeing the results of widespread drug availability and use in the 1960s and 1970s, the American public demanded action. The action they demanded, and upon which they still insist, is to attack drug trafficking and punish use. They have not accepted the false notion that addiction is a victimless crime; too many families have been destroyed for that fiction to carry much weight. They still believe in individual obligations to balance individual rights. They are not prepared to honor claims on the public treasury to substitute therapy for responsibility.

Policy makers have an obligation to respect those opinions and to take them into account. To go against such widely and deeply held convictions may be the mark of statesmanship in some circumstances. The public can be wrong; and when clear-sighted analysis based on convincing evidence is available, genuine leaders act upon it no matter how overwhelming the public sentiment. In this case, however, statesmanship is not required; good sense is.

The public is right.

Notes

1. Charles Murray, "How to Win the War on Drugs," *The New Republic*, May 21, 1990, pp. 19–25.
2. See John P. Walters, "How the Clinton Administration Is Abandoning the War Against Drugs," Heritage Foundation *Backgrounder* No. 989, June 16, 1994.
3. See Robert Peterson, "Legalization: The Myth Exposed," in Melvyn Krauss and Edward Lazear, eds., *Searching for Alternatives: Drug-Control Policy in the United States* (Stanford: Stanford University Press, 1991), pp. 324–355.
4. Milton Friedman, "An Open Letter to Bill Bennett," in Rod Evans and Irwin Berent, eds., *Drug Legalization: For and Against* (La Salle, IL: Open Court Press, 1992), pp. 49–52. For a more detailed expansion of this argument see also Friedman, "The War We Are Losing," *Searching for Alternatives*, pp. 53–68.
5. Mark Moore, "Actually, Prohibition Was a Success," *Drug Legalization*, pp. 95–97. For a counterargument, see John Morgan, "Prohibition Is Perverse Policy: What Was True in 1933 Is True Now," *Searching for Alternatives*, pp. 405–423.
6. This is not the place to discuss the requirements, intricacies, and liabilities of the appropriate use of analogies. Suffice it to say that, to be valid, there must be a respectable correspondence between the various elements of the analogy. An analogy works best when it is demonstrating parallels between lines of reasoning. It is far more dubious when used to argue that because A is so, by analogy, B must be so. Regardless of how close this correspondence is, an analogy is an illustration of a point, not a proof. It cannot substitute for facts.
7. See Ira Glasser, "Drug Prohibition: An Engine for Crime," *Searching for Alternatives*, pp. 271–282, for this argument in its most determined form.
8. One of the more breathless of these assertions holds that "We would be able to walk virtually any street at night as crime would be significantly reduced. Our criminal justice system would no longer be in gridlock. Our police could spend their time becoming members of the community. . . .

Courts would not be forced to plea-bargain. . . ." Kevin Zeese, "Drug War Forever?" *Searching for Alternatives*, pp. 251–268.

9. For a comprehensive review of these relationships, or the lack of causal links, see the definitive study by James Q. Wilson and Richard Herrnstein, *Crime and Human Nature* (New York: Touchstone Books, 1985); the various studies in Michael Tonry and James Q. Wilson, *Drugs and Crime* (Chicago: University of Chicago Press, 1990); and the studies in Mario De La Rosa et al., eds., *Drugs and Violence: Causes, Correlates, and Consequences*, NIDA Research Monograph 103 (Rockville, MD: NIDA, U.S. Department of Health and Human Services, 1990).
10. Mathea Falco, *The Making of a Drug-Free America: Programs That Work* (New York: Times Books, 1992), p. 9.
11. It should also be noted, contrary to Falco, that interdiction did virtually eliminate marijuana imports into the United States in the 1970s, and subsequent enforcement efforts have substantially raised, and kept uniformly high, street prices of what used to be a relatively cheap drug.
12. See Walters, "How the Clinton Administration Is Abandoning the War Against Drugs," p. 20.
13. *Ibid.*, p.21.
14. For a solid discussion of these efforts, see *Ibid.*, pp. 11–22.
15. Friedman, "An Open Letter," *Drug Legalization*, p. 50.
16. These figures are drawn from Bureau of Justice Statistics, *Sourcebook of Criminal Justice Statistics*, quoted in John Walters, "Race and the War on Drugs," an unpublished paper; and from *The Uniform Crime Reports: Crime in the United States, 1991* (United States Department of Justice, 1992), pp. 212–213.
17. "The US Government's 'War on Drugs' has become a war on drug users—a public moral crusade and law enforcement extravaganza that cordons off a rigid public policy from badly needed ideas and insights of medical and public health professionals who have spent a lifetime studying addiction, its causes and consequences." David Lewis, "Medical and Health Perspectives on a Failing US Drug Policy," *Daedalus*, 121 (Spring 1992), pp.165–194.
18. See Peter Reuter, "On the Consequences of Toughness," *Searching for Alternatives*, pp. 138–164, for an overview of the numbers.
19. Tom Morganthau and Mark Miller, "Tougher Law Enforcement Will Win the War on Drugs," in Neal Bernards, ed., *War on Drugs: Opposing Viewpoints* (San Diego, CA: Greenhaven Press, 1990), pp. 207–213.
20. Joel Hay, "The Harm They Do to Others: A Primer on the External Costs of Drug Abuse," *Searching for Alternatives*, pp. 200–225.
21. Surveys indicate that monthly cocaine use among non-addicts dropped almost 80 percent between 1985 and 1992. Annual use of illicit drugs by high school seniors dropped from 54.2 percent in 1979 to 27.1 percent in 1992. Indeed, in every category except hard-core abusers, there were significant declines in all types of drug use. See Walters, "How the Clinton Administration Is Abandoning the War Against Drugs," pp. 11–14.
22. See, for example, Steven Duke and Albert Gross, *America's Longest War* (New York: Putnam Books, 1993), Chapter 9, p. 160ff.

23. The argument that best underscores the fallacy in this type of reasoning is found in Thomas Sowell's various works, but most particularly in *Civil Rights: Rhetoric or Reality?* (New York: Quill, 1984) and *The Economics of Politics and Race* (New York: Quill, 1983).

24. See William Wilbanks, "The War on Drugs Is Not Racist," *War on Drugs: Opposing Viewpoints*, pp. 83–88.

25. See Nadelmann, "Beyond Drug Prohibition: Evaluating the Alternatives," *Searching for Alternatives*, pp. 241–250; "The Case for Legalization," *Drug Legalization*, pp. 19-26; and "Thinking Seriously About Alternatives to Drug Prohibition," *Daedalus* 121 (Spring 1992), pp. 53–84. Nadelmann's arguments are not atypical. The many other articles sympathetic to legalization and treatment-only policies in this issue of *Daedalus*, which focuses on rethinking drug policy, constitute a representative collection of views and arguments that mirror Nadelmann's views.

26. Nadelmann, "The Case for Legalization," p. 24.

27. Duke and Gross, *America's Longest War* (New York: Putnam Books, 1993), p. 2.

28. *Ibid.*, p. 5.

29. Robert Dupont, "Never Trust Anyone Under 40: What Employers Should Know About Drugs in the Workplace," *Policy Review* No. 48 (Spring 1989), pp. 52–57.

30. This wide range reflects different interpretations of the record. Lower figures tend to come from proponents, higher ones from opponents of legalization. See James Ostrowski, writing from the Cato Institute, "The Moral and Practical Case for Drug Legalization," *Hofstra Law Review* No. 18 (Spring 1990), pp. 607–702, quoted in Duke and Gross, *America's Longest War*, pp. 76–77 and endnote 119, on why the lower numbers are justified. For the rationale for higher numbers, see Morton Kondracke, "Don't Legalize Drugs: The Costs Are Still Too High," *Drug Legalization*, pp. 283–289.

31. Duke and Gross, *America's Longest War*, pp. 256–257. The authors see this as one of the examples justifying legalization.

32. See Peterson, "Legalization: The Myth Exposed," *Searching for Alternatives*, pp. 334–335.

33. Steven Wisotsky, "Statement of Steven Wisotsky Before the Select Committee on Narcotics Abuse and Control," in *Drug Legalization*, pp. 181–212.

34. This argument is made explicitly in David Lewis, "Medical and Health Perspectives on a Failing US Drug Policy," but is implicit in many others.

35. Zeese, "Drug War Forever?" *Searching for Alternatives*, p. 267.

36. In Falco's words, "We know that a drug-free America is within our grasp." This is so, she maintains, because of demand-control strategies. *Drug-Free America*, p. 202. Such a claim is, as most treatment advocates will agree, hyperbole. Even the most ardent legalization advocates do not argue that we would have a society totally free of drugs. But the assumption of a drug-free nation underlies the treatment-only position, which then is carried to extremes in order to sell it.

37. Zeese, "Drug War Forever?" *Searching for Alternatives*, p. 265.
38. This is a complex story with considerable bureaucratic battling over control or treatment. For a fuller account, see Horace Judson, *Heroin Addiction in Britain: What Americans Can Learn from the English Experience* (New York: Harcourt, 1982).
39. David Turner, "Pragmatic Incoherence: The Changing Face of British Drug Policy," *Searching for Alternatives*, pp. 173–190.
40. James Q. Wilson, "Against the Legalization of Drugs," *Drug Legalization*, pp. 26–45.
41. Because the sources vary wildly, these numbers represent averages.
42. John S. Mill, quoted in Lloyd Weinreb, *Natural Law and Justice* (Cambridge, MA: Harvard University Press, 1987), p. 135.
43. Hadley Arkes, *First Things: An Inquiry into the First Principles of Morals and Justice* (Princeton: Princeton University Press, 1986), pp. 415–416.
44. Wilson, "Against the Legalization of Drugs," *Drug Legalization*, pp. 40–41.
45. Todd Brenner, "The Legalization of Drugs: Why Prolong the Inevitable?" *Drug Legalization*, pp. 157–179.

10
The War on Drugs Is Not Futile

James Q. Wilson

James Q. Wilson is Collins Professor of Management and Public Policy at the University of California at Los Angeles. He is also the author of Thinking About Crime, Crime and Human Nature, *and* Bureaucracy.

Critics are wrong to argue that antidrug laws and efforts to enforce those laws have been unsuccessful. Since the 1970s, the criminal justice system has worked hard to enforce laws against drug trafficking, sales, possession, and use. It has succeeded in reducing the number of casual drug users significantly and in preventing much of the crime and chaos that coexist with the drug trade. Legalizing drugs would mean giving up the struggle against the harmful effects of drugs.

In 1972, the President appointed me chairman of the National Advisory Council for Drug Abuse Prevention. Created by Congress, the Council was charged with providing guidance on how best to coordinate the national war on drugs. (Yes, we called it a war then, too.) In those days, the drug we were chiefly concerned with was heroin. When I took office, heroin use had been increasing dramatically. Everybody was worried that this increase would continue. Such phrases as "heroin epidemic" were commonplace.

That same year, the eminent economist Milton Friedman published an essay in *Newsweek* in which he called for legalizing heroin. His argument was on two grounds: as a matter of ethics, the government has no right to tell people not to use heroin (or to drink or to commit suicide); as a matter of economics, the prohibition of drug use imposes costs on society that far exceed the benefits. Others, such as the psychoanalyst Thomas Szasz, made the same argument.

We did not take Friedman's advice. (Government commissions rarely do.) I do not recall that we even discussed legalizing heroin, though we did discuss (but did not take action on) legalizing a drug, cocaine, that

James Q. Wilson, "Against the Legalization of Drugs." Reprinted from *Commentary*, February 1990, by permission; all rights reserved.

many people then argued was benign. Our marching orders were to figure out how to win the war on heroin, not to run up the white flag of surrender.

That was 1972. Today, we have the same number of heroin addicts that we had then—half a million, give or take a few thousand. Having that many heroin addicts is no trivial matter; these people deserve our attention. But not having had an increase in that number for over fifteen years is also something that deserves our attention. What happened to the "heroin epidemic" that many people once thought would overwhelm us?

The facts are clear: a more or less stable pool of heroin addicts has been getting older, with relatively few new recruits. In 1976 the average age of heroin users who appeared in hospital emergency rooms was about twenty-seven; ten years later it was thirty-two. More than two-thirds of all heroin users appearing in emergency rooms are now over the age of thirty. Back in the early 1970's, when heroin got onto the national political agenda, the typical heroin addict was much younger, often a teenager. Household surveys show the same thing—the rate of opiate use (which includes heroin) has been flat for the better part of two decades. More fine-grained studies of inner-city neighborhoods confirm this. John Boyle and Ann Brunswick found that the percentage of young blacks in Harlem who used heroin fell from 8 percent in 1970–71 to about 3 percent in 1975–76.

Why did heroin lose its appeal for young people? When the young blacks in Harlem were asked why they stopped, more than half mentioned "trouble with the law" or "high cost" (and high cost is, of course, directly the result of law enforcement). Two-thirds said that heroin hurt their health; nearly all said they had had a bad experience with it. We need not rely, however, simply on what they said. In New York City in 1973–75, the street price of heroin rose dramatically and its purity sharply declined, probably as a result of the heroin shortage caused by the success of the Turkish government in reducing the supply of opium base and of the French government in closing down heroin-processing laboratories located in and around Marseilles. These were short-lived gains for, just as Friedman predicted, alternative sources of supply—mostly in Mexico—quickly emerged. But the three-year heroin shortage interrupted the easy recruitment of new users.

Today, we have the same number of heroin addicts that we had [in 1972]—half a million, give or take a few thousand.

Health and related problems were no doubt part of the reason for the reduced flow of recruits. Over the preceding years, Harlem youth had watched as more and more heroin users died of overdoses, were poisoned by adulterated doses, or acquired hepatitis from dirty needles. The word got around: heroin can kill you. By 1974 new hepatitis cases and drug-overdose deaths had dropped to a fraction of what they had been in 1970.

Alas, treatment did not seem to explain much of the cessation in drug use. Treatment programs can and do help heroin addicts, but treatment did not explain the drop in the number of *new* users (who by definition had never been in treatment) nor even much of the reduction in the number of experienced users.

No one knows how much of the decline to attribute to personal observation as opposed to high prices or reduced supply. But other evidence suggests strongly that price and supply played a large role. In 1972 the National Advisory Council was especially worried by the prospect that U.S. servicemen returning to this country from Vietnam would bring their heroin habits with them. Fortunately, a brilliant study by Lee Robins of Washington University in St. Louis put that fear to rest. She measured drug use of Vietnam veterans shortly after they had returned home. Though many had used heroin regularly while in Southeast Asia, most gave up the habit when back in the United States. The reason: here, heroin was less available and sanctions on its use were more pronounced. Of course, if a veteran had been willing to pay enough—which might have meant traveling to another city and would certainly have meant making an illegal contact with a disreputable dealer in a threatening neighborhood in order to acquire a (possibly) dangerous dose—he could have sustained his drug habit. Most veterans were unwilling to pay this price, and so their drug use declined or disappeared.

Reliving the past

Suppose we had taken Friedman's advice in 1972. What would have happened? We cannot be entirely certain, but at a minimum we would have placed the young heroin addicts (and, above all, the prospective addicts) in a very different position from the one in which they actually found themselves. Heroin would have been legal. Its price would have been reduced by 95 percent (minus whatever we chose to recover in taxes). Now that it could be sold by the same people who make aspirin, its quality would have been assured—no poisons, no adulterants. Sterile hypodermic needles would have been readily available at the neighborhood drugstore, probably at the same counter where the heroin was sold. No need to travel to big cities or unfamiliar neighborhoods—heroin could have been purchased anywhere, perhaps by mail order.

There would no longer have been any financial or medical reason to avoid heroin use. Anybody could have afforded it. We might have tried to prevent children from buying it, but as we have learned from our efforts to prevent minors from buying alcohol and tobacco, young people have a way of penetrating markets theoretically reserved for adults. Returning Vietnam veterans would have discovered that Omaha and Raleigh had been converted into the pharmaceutical equivalent of Saigon.

Under these circumstances, can we doubt for a moment that heroin use would have grown exponentially? Or that a vastly larger supply of new users would have been recruited? Professor Friedman is a Nobel Prize–winning economist whose understanding of market forces is profound. What did he think would happen to consumption under his legalized regime? Here are his words: "Legalizing drugs might increase the number of addicts, but it is not clear that it would. Forbidden fruit is attractive, particularly to the young."

Really? I suppose that we should expect no increase in Porsche sales if we cut the price by 95 percent, no increase in whiskey sales if we cut the price by a comparable amount—because young people only want fast cars and strong liquor when they are "forbidden." Perhaps Friedman's uncharacteristic lapse from the obvious implications of price theory can be explained by a misunderstanding of how drug users are recruited. In his 1972 essay he said that "drug addicts are deliberately made by pushers, who give likely prospects their first few doses free." If drugs were legal it would not pay anybody to produce addicts, because everybody would buy from the cheapest source. But as every drug expert knows, pushers do not produce addicts. Friends or acquaintances do. In fact, pushers are usually reluctant to deal with non-users because a non-user could be an undercover cop. Drug use spreads in the same way any fad or fashion spreads: somebody who is already a user urges his friends to try, or simply shows already-eager friends how to do it.

But we need not rely on speculation, however plausible, that lowered prices and more abundant supplies would have increased heroin usage. Great Britain once followed such a policy and with almost exactly those results. Until the mid-1960's, British physicians were allowed to prescribe heroin to certain classes of addicts. (Possessing these drugs without a doctor's prescription remained a criminal offense.) For many years this policy worked well enough because the addict patients were typically middle-class people who had become dependent on opiate painkillers while undergoing hospital treatment. There was no drug culture. The British system worked for many years, not because it prevented drug abuse, but because there was no problem of drug abuse that would test the system.

No one knows how much of the decline [in new heroin users] to attribute to personal observation as opposed to high prices or reduced supply.

All that changed in the 1960's. A few unscrupulous doctors began passing out heroin in wholesale amounts. One doctor prescribed almost 600,000 heroin tablets—that is, over thirteen pounds—in just one year. A youthful drug culture emerged with a demand for drugs far different from that of the older addicts. As a result, the British government required doctors to refer users to government-run clinics to receive their heroin.

But the shift to clinics did not curtail the growth in heroin use. Throughout the 1960's the number of addicts increased—the late John Kaplan of Stanford estimated by fivefold—in part as a result of the diversion of heroin from clinic patients to new users on the streets. An addict would bargain with the clinic doctor over how big a dose he would receive. The patient wanted as much as he could get, the doctor wanted to give as little as was needed. The patient had an advantage in this conflict because the doctor could not be certain how much was really needed. Many patients would use some of their "maintenance" dose and sell the remaining part to friends, thereby recruiting new addicts. As the clinics learned of this, they began to shift their treatment away from heroin and toward methadone, an addictive drug that, when taken orally, does not produce a "high" but will block the withdrawal pains associated with heroin abstinence.

Whether what happened in England in the 1960's was a mini-epidemic or an epidemic depends on whether one looks at numbers or at rates of change. Compared to the United States, the numbers were small. In 1960 there were 68 heroin addicts known to the British government; by 1968 there were 2,000 in treatment and many more who refused treatment. (They would refuse in part because they did not want to get methadone at a clinic if they could get heroin on the street.) Richard Hartnoll estimates that the actual number of addicts in England is five times the number officially registered. At a minimum, the number of British addicts increased by thirtyfold in ten years; the actual increase may have been much larger.

In the early 1980's the numbers began to rise again, and this time nobody doubted that a real epidemic was at hand. The increase was estimated to be 40 percent a year. By 1982 there were thought to be 20,000 heroin users in London alone. Geoffrey Pearson reports that many cities—Glasgow, Liverpool, Manchester, and Sheffield among them—were now experiencing a drug problem that once had been largely confined to London. The problem, again, was supply. The country was being flooded with cheap, high-quality heroin, first from Iran and then from Southeast Asia.

The United States began the 1960's with a much larger number of heroin addicts and probably a bigger at-risk population than was the case in Great Britain. Even though it would be foolhardy to suppose that the British system, if installed here, would have worked the same way or with the same results, it would be equally foolhardy to suppose that a combination of heroin available from leaky clinics and from street dealers who faced only minimal law-enforcement risks would not have produced a much greater increase in heroin use than we actually experienced. My guess is that if we had allowed either doctors or clinics to prescribe heroin, we would have had far worse results than were produced in Britain, if for no other reason than the vastly larger number of addicts with which we began. We would have had to find some way to police thousands (not scores) of physicians and hundreds (not dozens) of clinics. If the British civil service found it difficult to keep heroin in the hands of addicts and out of the hands of recruits when it was dealing with a few hundred people, how well would the American civil service have accomplished the same tasks when dealing with tens of thousands of people?

Back to the future

Now cocaine, especially in its potent form, crack, is the focus of attention. Now as in 1972 the government is trying to reduce its use. Now as then some people are advocating legalization. Is there any more reason to yield to those arguments today than there was almost two decades ago?[1]

I think not. If we had yielded in 1972 we almost certainly would have had today a permanent population of several million, not several hundred thousand, heroin addicts. If we yield now we will have a far more serious problem with cocaine.

Crack is worse than heroin by almost any measure. Heroin produces a pleasant drowsiness and, if hygienically administered, has only the physical side effects of constipation and sexual impotence. Regular heroin use incapacitates many users, especially poor ones, for any productive work or social responsibility. They will sit nodding on a street corner, helpless but at least harmless. By contrast, regular cocaine use leaves the user neither helpless nor harmless. When smoked (as with crack) or injected, cocaine produces instant, intense, and short-lived euphoria. The experience generates a powerful desire to repeat it. If the drug is readily available, repeat use will occur. Those people who progress to "bingeing" on cocaine become devoted to the drug and its effects to the exclusion of almost all other considerations—job, family, children, sleep, food, even sex. Dr. Frank Gawin at Yale and Dr. Everett Ellinwood at Duke report that a substantial percentage of all high-dose, binge users become uninhibited, impulsive, hypersexual, compulsive, irritable, and hyperactive. Their moods vacillate dramatically, leading at times to violence and homicide.

If we had yielded in 1972 we almost certainly would have had today a permanent population of several million, not several hundred thousand, heroin addicts.

Women are much more likely to use crack than heroin, and if they are pregnant, the effects on their babies are tragic. Douglas Besharov, who has been following the effects of drugs on infants for twenty years, writes that nothing he learned about heroin prepared him for the devastation of cocaine. Cocaine harms the fetus and can lead to physical deformities or neurological damage. Some crack babies have for all practical purposes suffered a disabling stroke while still in the womb. The long-term consequences of this brain damage are lowered cognitive ability and the onset of mood disorders. Besharov estimates that about 30,000 to 50,000 such babies are born every year, about 7,000 in New York City alone. There may be ways to treat such infants, but from everything we now know the treatment will be long, difficult, and expensive. Worse, the mothers who are most likely to produce crack babies are precisely the ones who, because of poverty or temperament, are least able and willing to obtain such treatment. In fact, anecdotal evidence suggests that crack mothers are likely to abuse their infants.

The notion that abusing drugs such as cocaine is a "victimless crime" is not only absurd but dangerous. Even ignoring the fetal drug syndrome, crack-dependent people are, like heroin addicts, individuals who regularly victimize their children by neglect, their spouses by improvidence, their employers by lethargy, and their coworkers by carelessness. Society is not and could never be a collection of autonomous individuals. We all have a stake in ensuring that each of us displays a minimal level of dignity, responsibility, and empathy. We cannot, of course, coerce people into goodness, but we can and should insist that some standards must be met if society itself—on which the very existence of the human personality depends—is to persist. Drawing the line that defines those standards is difficult and contentious, but if crack and heroin use do not fall below it, what does?

The advocates of legalization will respond by suggesting that my picture is overdrawn. Ethan Nadelmann of Princeton argues that the risk of legalization is less than most people suppose. Over 20 million Americans between the ages of eighteen and twenty-five have tried cocaine (according to a government survey), but only a quarter million use it daily. From this Nadelmann concludes that at most 3 percent of all young people who try cocaine develop a problem with it. The implication is clear: make the drug legal and we only have to worry about 3 percent of our youth.

The implication rests on a logical fallacy and a factual error. The fallacy is this: the percentage of occasional cocaine users who become binge users *when the drug is illegal* (and thus expensive and hard to find) tells us nothing about the percentage who will become dependent when the drug is legal (and thus cheap and abundant). Drs. Gawin and Ellinwood report, in common with several other researchers, that controlled or occasional use of cocaine changes to compulsive and frequent use "when access to the drug increases" or when the user switches from snorting to smoking. More cocaine more potently administered alters, perhaps sharply, the proportion of "controlled" users who become heavy users.

The factual error is this: the federal survey Nadelmann quotes was done in 1985, *before* crack had become common. Thus the probability of becoming dependent on cocaine was derived from the responses of users who snorted the drug. The speed and potency of cocaine's action increases dramatically when it is smoked. We do not yet know how greatly the advent of crack increases the risk of dependency, but all the clinical evidence suggests that the increase is likely to be large.

It is possible that some people will not become heavy users even when the drug is readily available in its most potent form. So far there are no scientific grounds for predicting who will and who will not become dependent. Neither socioeconomic background nor personality traits differentiates between casual and intensive users. Thus, the only way to settle the question of who is correct about the effect of easy availability on drug use, Nadelmann or Gawin and Ellinwood, is to try it and see. But that social experiment is so risky as to be no experiment at all, for if cocaine is legalized and if the rate of its abusive use increases dramatically, there is no way to put the genie back in the bottle, and it is not a kindly genie.

Have we lost?

Many people who agree that there are risks in legalizing cocaine or heroin still favor it because, they think, we have lost the war on drugs. "Nothing we have done has worked" and the current federal policy is just "more of the same." Whatever the costs of greater drug use, surely they would be less than the costs of our present, failed efforts.

That is exactly what I was told in 1972—and heroin is not quite as bad a drug as cocaine. We did not surrender and we did not lose. We did not win, either. What the nation accomplished then was what most efforts to save people from themselves accomplish: the problem was contained and the number of victims minimized, all at a considerable cost in law enforcement and increased crime. Was the cost worth it? I think so, but others may disagree. What are the lives of would-be addicts worth? I recall some people saying to me then, "Let them kill themselves." I was appalled. Happily, such views did not prevail.

Have we lost today? Not at all. High-rate cocaine use is not commonplace. The National Institute of Drug Abuse (NIDA) reports that less than 5 percent of high-school seniors used cocaine within the last thirty days. Of course this survey misses young people who have dropped out of school and miscounts those who lie on the questionnaire, but even if we inflate the NIDA estimate by some plausible percentage, it is still not much above 5 percent. Medical examiners reported in 1987 that about 1,500 died from cocaine use; hospital emergency rooms reported about 30,000 admissions related to cocaine abuse.

The notion that abusing drugs such as cocaine is a "victimless crime" is not only absurd but dangerous.

These are not small numbers, but neither are they evidence of a nationwide plague that threatens to engulf us all. Moreover, cities vary greatly in the proportion of people who are involved with cocaine. To get city-level data we need to turn to drug tests carried out on arrested persons, who obviously are more likely to be drug users than the average citizen. The National Institute of Justice, through its Drug Use Forecasting (DUF) project, collects urinalysis data on arrestees in 22 cities. As we have already seen, opiate (chiefly heroin) use has been flat or declining in most of these cities since the 1980's. Cocaine use has gone up sharply, but with great variation among cities. New York, Philadelphia, and Washington, D.C., all report that two-thirds or more of their arrestees tested positive for cocaine, but in Portland, San Antonio, and Indianapolis the percentage was one-third or less.

In some neighborhoods, of course, matters have reached crisis proportions. Gangs control the streets, shootings terrorize residents, and drug-dealing occurs in plain view. The police seem barely able to contain matters. But in these neighborhoods—unlike at Palo Alto cocktail parties—the people are not calling for legalization, they are calling for help. And often not much help has come. Many cities are willing to do almost anything about the drug problem except spend more money on it. The federal government cannot change that; only local voters and politicians can. It is not clear that they will.

It took about ten years to contain heroin. We have had experience with crack for only [a few] years. Each year we spend perhaps $11 billion on law enforcement (and some of that goes to deal with marijuana) and perhaps $2 billion on treatment. Large sums, but not sums that should lead anyone to say, "We just can't afford this any more."

The illegality of drugs increases crime, partly because some users turn to crime to pay for their habits, partly because some users are stimulated by certain drugs (such as crack or PCP) to act more violently or ruthlessly than they otherwise would, and partly because criminal organizations seeking to control drug supplies use force to manage their markets. These also are serious costs, but no one knows how much they would be reduced if drugs were legalized. Addicts would no longer steal to pay black-market prices for drugs, a real gain. But some, perhaps a great deal, of that gain would be offset by the great increase in the number of addicts. These people, nodding on heroin or living in the delusion-ridden high of cocaine, would hardly be ideal employees. Many would steal simply to support themselves, since snatch-and-grab, opportunistic crime can be managed even by people unable to hold a regular job or plan an elaborate crime. Those British addicts who get their supplies from government clinics are not models of law-abiding decency. Most are in crime, and though their per-capita rate of criminality may be lower thanks to the cheapness of their drugs, the total volume of crime they produce may be quite large. Of course, society could decide to support all unemployable addicts on welfare, but that would mean that gains from lowered rates of crime would have to be offset by large increases in welfare budgets.

Proponents of legalization claim that the costs of having more addicts around would be largely if not entirely offset by having more money available with which to treat and care for them. The money would come from taxes levied on the sale of heroin and cocaine.

To obtain this fiscal dividend, however, legalization's supporters must first solve an economic dilemma. If they want to raise a lot of money to pay for welfare and treatment, the tax rate on the drugs will have to be quite high. Even if they themselves do not want a high rate, the politicians' love of "sin taxes" would probably guarantee that it would be high anyway. But the higher the tax, the higher the price of the drug, and the higher the price the greater the likelihood that addicts will turn to crime to find the money for it and that criminal organizations will be formed to sell tax-free drugs at below-market rates. If we managed to keep taxes (and thus prices) low, we would get that much less money to pay for welfare and treatment and more people could afford to become addicts. There may be an optimal tax rate for drugs that maximizes revenue while minimizing crime, bootlegging, and the recruitment of new addicts, but our experience with alcohol does not suggest that we know how to find it.

The benefits of illegality

The advocates of legalization find nothing to be said in favor of the current system except, possibly, that it keeps the number of addicts smaller than it would otherwise be. In fact, the benefits are more substantial than that.

First, treatment. All the talk about providing "treatment on demand" implies that there is a demand for treatment. That is not quite right. There are some drug-dependent people who genuinely want treatment and will remain in it if offered; they should receive it. But there are far more who want only short-term help after a bad crash; once stabilized and bathed, they are back on the street again, hustling. And even many of the addicts who enroll in a program honestly wanting help drop out after a short while when they discover that help takes time and commitment. Drug-dependent people have very short time horizons and a weak capacity for commitment. These two groups—those looking for a quick fix and those unable to stick with a long-term fix—are not easily helped.

Even if we increase the number of treatment slots—as we should—we would have to do something to make treatment more effective.

One thing that can often make it more effective is compulsion. Douglas Anglin of UCLA, in common with many other researchers, has found that the longer one stays in a treatment program, the better the chances of a reduction in drug dependency. But he, again like most other researchers, has found that drop-out rates are high. He has also found, however, that patients who enter treatment under legal compulsion stay in the program longer than those not subject to such pressure. His research on the California civil-commitment program, for example, found that heroin users involved with its required drug-testing program had over the long term a lower rate of heroin use than similar addicts who were free of such constraints. If for many addicts compulsion is a useful component of treatment, it is not clear how compulsion could be achieved in a society in which purchasing, possessing, and using the drug were legal. It could be managed, I suppose, but I would not want to have to answer the challenge from the American Civil Liberties Union that it is wrong to compel a person to undergo treatment for consuming a legal commodity.

Once a drug is legal, not only will its use increase but many of those who then use it will prefer the drug to the treatment.

Next, education. We are now investing substantially in drug-education programs in the schools. Though we do not yet know for certain what will work, there are some promising leads. But I wonder how credible such programs would be if they were aimed at dissuading children from doing something perfectly legal. We could, of course, treat drug education like smoking education: inhaling crack and inhaling tobacco are both legal, but you should not do it because it is bad for you. That tobacco is bad for you is easily shown; the Surgeon General has seen to that. But what do we say about crack? It is pleasurable, but devoting yourself to so much pleasure is not a good idea (though perfectly legal)? Unlike tobacco, cocaine will not give you cancer or emphysema, but it will lead you to neglect your duties to family, job, and neighborhood? Everybody is doing cocaine, but you should not?

Again, it might be possible under a legalized regime to have effective drug-prevention programs, but their effectiveness would depend heavily, I think, on first having decided that cocaine use, like tobacco use, is purely a matter of practical consequences; no fundamental moral significance attaches to either. But if we believe—as I do—that dependency on certain mind-altering drugs *is* a moral issue and that their illegality rests in part on their immorality, then legalizing them undercuts, if it does not eliminate altogether, the moral message.

That message is at the root of the distinction we now make between nicotine and cocaine. Both are highly addictive; both have harmful physical effects. But we treat the two drugs differently, not simply because nicotine is so widely used as to be beyond the reach of effective prohibition, but because its use does not destroy the user's essential humanity.

Tobacco shortens one's life, cocaine debases it. Nicotine alters one's habits, cocaine alters one's soul. The heavy use of crack, unlike the heavy use of tobacco, corrodes those natural sentiments of sympathy and duty that constitute our human nature and make possible our social life. To say, as does Nadelmann, that distinguishing morally between tobacco and cocaine is "little more than a transient prejudice" is close to saying that morality itself is but a prejudice.

The alcohol problem

Now we have arrived where many arguments about legalizing drugs begin: is there any reason to treat heroin and cocaine differently from the way we treat alcohol?

There is no easy answer to that question because, as with so many human problems, one cannot decide simply on the basis either of moral principles or of individual consequences; one has to temper any policy by a common-sense judgment of what is possible. Alcohol, like heroin, cocaine, PCP, and marijuana, is a drug—that is, a mood-altering substance—and consumed to excess it certainly has harmful consequences: auto accidents, barroom fights, bedroom shootings. It is also, for some people, addictive. We cannot confidently compare the addictive powers of these drugs, but the best evidence suggests that crack and heroin are much more addictive than alcohol.

Many people, Nadelmann included, argue that since the health and financial costs of alcohol abuse are so much higher than those of cocaine or heroin abuse, it is hypocritical folly to devote our efforts to preventing cocaine or drug use. But as Mark Kleiman of Harvard has pointed out, this comparison is quite misleading. What Nadelmann is doing is showing that a *legalized* drug (alcohol) produces greater social harm than *illegal* ones (cocaine and heroin). But of course. Suppose that in the 1920's we had made heroin and cocaine legal and alcohol illegal. Can anyone doubt that Nadelmann would now be writing that it is folly to continue our ban on alcohol because cocaine and heroin are so much more harmful?

And let there be no doubt about it—widespread heroin and cocaine use are associated with all manner of ills. Thomas Bewley found that the mortality rate of British heroin addicts in 1968 was 28 times as high as the death rate of the same age group of non-addicts, even though in England at the time an addict could obtain free or low-cost heroin and clean needles from British clinics. Perform the following mental experiment: suppose we legalized heroin and cocaine in this country. In what proportion of auto fatalities would the state police report that the driver was nodding off on heroin or recklessly driving on a coke high? In what proportion of spouse-assault and child-abuse cases would the local police report that crack was involved? In what proportion of industrial accidents would safety investigators report that the forklift or drill-press operator was in a drug-induced stupor or frenzy? We do not know exactly what the proportion would be, but anyone who asserts that it would not be much higher than it is now would have to believe that these drugs have little appeal except when they are illegal. And that is nonsense.

An advocate of legalization might concede that social harm—perhaps harm equivalent to that already produced by alcohol—would follow from making cocaine and heroin generally available. But at least, he might add, we would have the problem "out in the open" where it could be treated as a matter of "public health." That is well and good, if we knew how to treat—that is, cure—heroin and cocaine abuse. But we do not know how to do it for all the people who would need such help. We are having only limited success in coping with chronic alcoholics. Addictive behavior is immensely difficult to change, and the best methods for changing it—living in drug-free therapeutic communities, becoming faithful members of Alcoholics Anonymous or Narcotics Anonymous—require great personal commitment, a quality that is, alas, in short supply among the very persons—young people, disadvantaged people—who are often most at risk for addiction.

[If drugs were more accessible] the result would be a sharp increase in use, a more widespread degradation of the human personality, and a greater rate of accidents and violence.

Suppose that today we had not 15 million alcohol abusers, but half a million. Suppose that we already knew what we have learned from our long experience with the widespread use of alcohol. Would we make whiskey legal? I do not know, but I suspect there would be a lively debate. The Surgeon General would remind us of the risks alcohol poses to pregnant women. The National Highway Traffic Safety Administration would point to the likelihood of more highway fatalities caused by drunk drivers. The Food and Drug Administration might find that there is a nontrivial increase in cancer associated with alcohol consumption. At the same time the police would report great difficulty in keeping illegal whiskey out of our cities, officers being corrupted by bootleggers, and alcohol addicts often resorting to crime to feed their habit. Libertarians, for their part, would argue that every citizen has a right to drink anything he wishes and that drinking is, in any event, a "victimless crime."

However the debate might turn out, the central fact would be that the problem was still, at that point, a small one. The government cannot legislate away the addictive tendencies in all of us, nor can it remove completely even the most dangerous addictive substances. But it can cope with harms when the harms are still manageable.

Science and addiction

One advantage of containing a problem while it is still containable is that it buys time for science to learn more about it and perhaps to discover a cure. Almost unnoticed in the current debate over legalizing drugs is that basic science has made rapid strides in identifying the underlying neurological processes involved in some forms of addiction. Stimulants such as cocaine and amphetamines alter the way certain brain cells communicate with one another. That alteration is complex and not entirely understood, but in simplified form it involves modifying the way in which a neurotransmitter called dopamine sends signals from one cell to another.

When dopamine crosses the synapse between two cells, it is in effect carrying a message from the first cell to activate the second one. In certain parts of the brain that message is experienced as pleasure. After the message is delivered, the dopamine returns to the first cell. Cocaine apparently blocks this return, or "reuptake," so that the excited cell and others nearby continue to send pleasure messages. When the exaggerated high produced by cocaine-influenced dopamine finally ends, the brain cells may (in ways that are still a matter of dispute) suffer from an extreme lack of dopamine, thereby making the individual unable to experience any pleasure at all. This would explain why cocaine users often feel so depressed after enjoying the drug. Stimulants may also affect the way in which other neurotransmitters, such as serotonin and noradrenaline, operate.

Whatever the exact mechanism may be, once it is identified it becomes possible to use drugs to block either the effect of cocaine or its tendency to produce dependency. There have already been experiments using desipramine, imipramine, bromocriptine, carbamazepine, and other chemicals. There are some promising results.

Tragically, we spend very little on such research, and the agencies funding it have not in the past occupied very influential or visible posts in the federal bureaucracy. If there is one aspect of the "war on drugs" metaphor that I dislike, it is its tendency to focus attention almost exclusively on the troops in the trenches, whether engaged in enforcement or treatment, and away from the research-and-development efforts back on the home front where the war may ultimately be decided.

I believe that the prospects of scientists in controlling addiction will be strongly influenced by the size and character of the problem they face. If the problem is a few hundred thousand chronic, high-dose users of an illegal product, the chances of making a difference at a reasonable cost will be much greater than if the problem is a few million chronic users of legal substances. Once a drug is legal, not only will its use increase but many of those who then use it will prefer the drug to the treatment: they will want the pleasure, whatever the cost to themselves or their families, and they will resist—probably successfully—any effort to wean them away from experiencing the high that comes from inhaling a legal substance.

If I am wrong . . .

No one can know what our society would be like if we changed the law to make access to cocaine, heroin, and PCP easier. I believe, for reasons given, that the result would be a sharp increase in use, a more widespread degradation of the human personality, and a greater rate of accidents and violence.

I may be wrong. If I am, then we will needlessly have incurred heavy costs in law enforcement and some forms of criminality. But if I am right, and the legalizers prevail anyway, then we will have consigned millions of people, hundreds of thousands of infants, and hundreds of neighborhoods to a life of oblivion and disease. To the lives and families destroyed by alcohol we will have added countless more destroyed by cocaine, heroin, PCP, and whatever else a basement scientist can invent.

Human character is formed by society; indeed, human character is inconceivable without society, and good character is less likely in a bad society. Will we, in the name of an abstract doctrine of radical individualism, and with the false comfort of suspect predictions, decide to take the chance that somehow individual decency can survive amid a more general level of degradation?

I think not. The American people are too wise for that, whatever the academic essayists and cocktail-party pundits may say. But if Americans today are less wise than I suppose, then Americans at some future time will look back on us now and wonder, what kind of people were they that they could have done such a thing?

Notes

1. I do not here take up the question of marijuana. For a variety of reasons—its widespread use and its lesser tendency to addict—it presents a different problem from cocaine or heroin. For a penetrating analysis, see Mark Kleiman, *Marijuana: Costs of Abuse, Costs of Control*, Greenwood Press.

11

Legalizing Drugs Would Not Reduce Crime

Gerald W. Lynch and Roberta Blotner

Gerald W. Lynch is president of the John Jay College of Criminal Justice, a unit of the City University of New York (CUNY). Roberta Blotner is the director of CUNY's substance-abuse prevention programs.

Proponents of drug legalization are wrong to argue that legalizing drugs would eliminate the crime and violence that surround the illegal drug trade. If drugs were legalized, drug use would increase—and so would the crimes commonly associated with drug abuse. Rather than legalizing drugs, society should develop programs to prevent drug abuse, offer treatment to drug addicts, and maintain strict laws against illegal drugs.

In "The Challenge of Legalizing Drugs," Joseph P. Kane, S.J., in the August 8, 1992 *America*, presents a compelling description of the devastation wreaked on our society by drug abuse, but draws some troubling conclusions supporting the legalization of drugs. Father Kane argues that illegal drugs promote the proliferation of crime because of the huge profits associated with their import and sales. Violence and murder have increased dramatically as dealers and gangs compete for turf and drug profits. Youngsters are attracted to selling drugs in order to earn more money than they could ever hope to earn in legitimate jobs. Addicts steal to pay for their drugs. The criminal justice system is overwhelmed by the increasing number of drug arrests.

He further argues that because drugs are illegal, addicts are treated as criminals rather than as sick people in need of help. Addicts are often arrested and processed through the criminal justice system rather than offered legitimate rehabilitation or treatment. Finally, he states that illegal drugs exploit the poor, whose struggle to survive makes drug dealing a sometimes necessary alternative.

The solution to the problem, he concludes, is to legalize drugs while at the same time 1) changing attitudes within our society about drugs, 2) changing laws and public policy, and 3) providing drug education and

Gerald W. Lynch and Roberta Blotner, "Legalizing Drugs Is Not the Solution," *America*, February 13, 1993. Reprinted with permission.

treatment to all those who want it. While Father Kane's description of the toll drugs are taking on our society and our citizens is poignant, the solution to this problem is not legalization.

Legalizing drugs will almost certainly increase their use. This has been well documented in a number of studies. J. F. Mosher points out that alcohol usage and rates of liver disease declined significantly during Prohibition ("Drug Availability in a Public Health Perspective" in *Youth and Drugs: Society's Mixed Messages* [1990]). Moreover, following repeal of the 18th Amendment, the number of drinkers in the United States increased by 60 percent.

The most widely abused drugs in our society are tobacco, alcohol and prescription drugs—the legal drugs and those which are most widely available. A recent report issued by the Federal Government states that approximately 57 million people in this country are addicted to cigarettes, 18 million are addicted to alcohol and 10 million are abusing psychotherapeutic drugs. By comparison, crack, heroin and hallucinogens each account for one million addicts. Further, the report states that every day in this country 1,000 people die of smoking-related illnesses, 550 die of alcohol-related accidents and diseases, while 20 die of drug overdoses and drug-related homicides. In addition, the annual costs of health care and lost productivity to employers are estimated at $600 billion for alcoholism and $60 billion for tobacco-related ailments. For all illegal drugs, however, the comparable cost is an estimated $40 billion (see "Making America Drug Free: A New Vision of What Works," *Carnegie Quarterly* [Summer 1992]). These data clearly demonstrate that the drugs which are most available are the most abused, the most dangerous and the most costly.

As the number of people using drugs increases, babies born to addicted mothers will increase as well. According to a report issued by the New York City Public Schools in 1991, during the preceding 10 years babies born to substance-abusing mothers increased 3,000 percent. It is estimated that each year approximately 10,000 babies are born exposed to drugs. With greater availability of drugs, it is inevitable that more babies will be born to substance-abusing mothers. According to guidelines offered by the Children Prenatally Exposed to Drugs Program of the Los Angeles Unified School District, the following are among the characteristics of the child prenatally exposed to drugs: neurological problems, affective disorders, poor concentration, delayed language development, impaired social skills, difficulty in play. The extent to which children of addicted fathers may be impaired is not yet known. Legalizing drugs will surely compound the tragedy to our society of these most innocent victims.

Drugs and crime

Drug legalization would not eliminate crime. Although crimes associated with obtaining drugs might decrease with legalization, other crimes, especially violent crimes, would increase. As many as 80 percent of violent crimes involve alcohol and drugs. A number of studies have demonstrated the relationship between drugs and homicides, automobile deaths, child abuse and sexual abuse. It is estimated that drugs and alcohol are involved in 50 percent to 75 percent of cases of suicidal behavior. According to recent pharmacological research, certain drugs, especially cocaine, have the tendency to elicit violent behavior because of changes that take place in the neurotransmitter systems of the brain.

Many experts think that unless there were free access to unlimited quantities of drugs, there would be a black market even after legalization. Drugs, even if legal, would still cost money. Since many addicts cannot maintain jobs, they would continue to engage in stealing and prostitution to pay for drugs and would continue to subject their families and friends to abuse.

Legalizing drugs will almost certainly increase their use.

Experiments with the decriminalization of drugs have failed. A case in point is Zurich, Switzerland. There the city set aside a park, the Platzspitz, in which drugs were decriminalized and were available with no legal consequences. Health care was made accessible and clean syringes were supplied. It was hoped that there would be a reduction in crime, better health care for addicts and containment of the problem to a defined area of the city. The experiment failed dramatically.

As reported in the *New York Times* on February 11, 1992, and London's *Financial Times* on January 4, 1992, Zurich's drug-related crime and violence actually increased. Drug users and dealers converged on the Swiss city from other countries throughout Europe. The health-care system was overwhelmed as drug users had to be resuscitated. As drug dealers began to compete for business, the cost of drugs decreased. One addict was quoted as saying, "Too many kids were getting hooked too easily." The Platzspitz, a garden spot in the center of Zurich, was devastated. Statues were marred with graffiti. The ground was littered with used syringes and soaked with urine. Citizens avoided the area and the city finally ended its experiment. The park was closed and surrounded by a high fence to keep out the drug addicts and dealers. Plans are now being implemented to renovate the park and restore its original beauty. Zurich has served as a real-life experiment that proves the failure of decriminalization.

We believe that we must change public attitudes toward drugs and focus on prevention and treatment, but we must also maintain the laws making drugs illegal. A goal of prevention is to create an environment that rejects drug use and dealing. Effective prevention involves a comprehensive approach that includes the following components: education, including information about drugs; helping children understand the pressures from friends, family and school that may promote the use of drugs; social-competency skills to assist them in resisting the temptations of drugs; making available intervention (counseling, treatment) to those who have begun to use drugs; promoting positive alternatives to drug use; providing training to those who relate to children and influencing social policies (see *An Assessment of Substance Abuse Prevention*, New York State Division of Substance Abuse Services, October 1989).

Effective prevention efforts also attempt to promote negative attitudes toward drug use by communicating clear, consistent anti-substance-abuse messages through the mass media, within communities and in educational settings. A final important prevention strategy is to enforce stringently the laws against illegal drugs in order to control their availability.

When community prevention efforts are coupled with strong and decisive national leadership, the chances for change are greatly enhanced. Perhaps the most dramatic examples of the effectiveness of these partnerships are the anti–drunk driving and anti-smoking campaigns. These campaigns grew out of public intolerance of problems that not only plagued their communities, but decimated their children. Volunteers, community activists, parents and youth groups organized, developed community prevention strategies and applied unrelenting pressure on public officials, the private sector and the media. These activists were influential in shifting public attitudes. At the same time, Federal as well as state and local officials passed laws and changed public policies to regulate smoking in public areas, limit advertising and increase drunk-driving penalties. The result has been fewer traffic fatalities and a decrease in the social acceptability of drunk driving and smoking.

A study conducted by the New York State Division of Substance Abuse Services in 1990 found that during the preceding 12 years marijuana, cocaine and alcohol use had declined among school-age children. National data show similar trends. Studies of high school seniors conducted over the past decade have shown a dramatic decline in drug use as well. Legalizing drugs now would only send a confused message that could be interpreted as implying that the Government condones their use.

Drug legalization would not eliminate crime.

While legalization may appear to be a realistic solution to a very difficult problem, it would be a tremendous mistake. With legalization would come an increase in availability of drugs and an increase in the problems associated with their abuse: the suffering of addicts and their loved ones; the death and loss of thousands of innocent lives; great costs to society, to the health-care system, to employers, and, above all, social, economic and emotional costs to our children.

Instead of legalizing drugs, we must devote massive resources to education and treatment. We must communicate the clear and consistent message that drugs are destructive and will not be tolerated. We must so change public policy and attitudes that every addict who wants treatment can receive it. We must continue to use our resources to enforce the laws against drugs in order to keep drugs out of our communities. Rather than giving up the fight and legalizing drugs, it is crucial that we redouble our efforts to solve the problem.

12
Legalizing Drugs Would Increase Drug Abuse

A.M. Rosenthal

A.M. Rosenthal is a regular editorialist for the New York Times.

Legalizing drugs would be cruel. If drugs were legal, then more people would use them and, of course, become addicted to them. More babies will be born addicted to the drugs their mothers abused, more children will be abused, and more lives will be ruined if drugs are legalized.

The campaign for drug legalization grows in wallet and prestige. But, as it picks up journalistic and academic endorsement and foundation money, one thing stays constant. It remains now, as it always has been, one of the most cruel and selfish movements in America.

The great majority of Americans are against legalization. So are the politicians they elect to office.

And Americans who believe in using government power and public opinion to fight narcotics are drowsily inclined to believe that to pay attention to the legalization movement would strengthen it, so let's not.

While we slumber, the movement becomes respectable. The Soros foundation recently gave pro-legalizers at least $6 million, to study legalization and decriminalization.

Meanwhile, the struggle against drugs is long and wearying. Achievement does not always hold steady. People who say they have a cheap and fast solution get a hearing their logic would never earn them.

Far more important, it is clear that the legalizers can make important headway without passing laws. They strive to weaken the essential national resolve that the drug war must be fought with as many weapons and for as long as it takes.

This is backdoor drug acceptance, almost as dangerous as legalization. The U.S. is still paying in broken lives, fear, violence and damaged newborns for the tacit decriminalization won by the counterculture in the 60's.

In December 1994 the University of Michigan Institute for Social Research reported that illegal drug use among secondary school students is rising. The study traced an expansion of drug use among young people into the late 1970's, a decline through 1991 and since then a resurgence.

The warning from the study group was that as children heard less disapproval and more glamorization or approval of drugs, their own use went up. You don't really need a law.

It is time to state the truth, as often as the message is heard in the academy, the press, the movies or TV. The legalization movement is cruel because it would create more addicts, more abused children, more victims of muggings and robbery, millions more every single year.

It is selfish because it would move the entire burden of fighting drugs from the totality of society to neighborhoods that already suffer most. It is both cruel and selfish because it glides over the ruined lives of those who abuse drugs, legally or not.

The movement claims that legalization would drive drug mobsters out of business, which would cut down on crime so us non-addicts could live in peace. But nobody has demonstrated how it would reduce crime or addiction, because it will not.

Police enforcement

Mayor Rudolph Giuliani and the New York police have shown the way at least to cut down on drug-mob shootings. Go after them, arrest gunners, pushers and their customers; don't look away, put them away.

The police have done their job well enough in Washington Heights to force the mobsters indoors. That cuts down on street assassinations. But it has not cut down on drug abuse, or on crimes by addicts.

Most drug crimes are not carried out by addicts frantic for drug buying money, but after and because of drug use, by addicts who take to cold-blooded crime as the only way drugs leave them fit to make a living.

If legalization made drugs purchasable without penalty—or gave them away—there would be more addicts, therefore more crime. That is the root hoax of legalization.

To fight drugs and drug crime takes a combination of interdiction at home and abroad, well-funded drug therapy and a resolute anti-drug national consensus enforced by tough, constant parent, police and neighborhood pressure. A combination.

Americans who support legalization are not looking for an up or down vote. They know they could never win. But they also know, because America has seen it happen, that if the public stops caring about enforcing the drug laws, that is just as good as taking them off the books, and a lot less trouble.

Americans who support drug legalization or decriminalization may be otherwise decent people. But to the extent they succeed they are responsible for what is wrought, even though they be lovely to their own children and house plants, and whether they contribute one dollar or six million, in coin or embrace.

13

The Benefits of Drug Legalization Are Myths

Lee P. Brown

Lee P. Brown, a former police chief, is the director of national drug control policy for the Clinton administration.

Advocates proclaim that legalizing drugs would benefit American society by reducing crime and drug abuse. This is untrue. Violence and drug abuse would continue and even increase if drugs were legalized. Reducing the availability of drugs, preventing drug abuse, and treating addicts are needed to address the drug problem in the United States.

Let me say immediately that I am very pleased to have been invited to talk to this conference on drug policy and drug policy reform [of the Civil Liberties Union of Massachusetts]—to an audience whose members have serious questions about the direction of national policy, and who are prepared to hear what we have to say about it.

As I look around me, I know that I am speaking to many who believe that our country's drug policy must be radically changed. To them, what I say here may not be convenient, or particularly easy. But it must be said.

The use of drugs, and the causes and consequences of drug use, are serious matters. They affect us all. To me, and to the Clinton Administration, drug use is among the most important domestic issues that our nation faces.

The use of illegal drugs is a very complex policy issue. It goes to the core of our behavior as individuals, as families, as communities, and as a nation. It has global implications. Those of us who must grapple daily with the issue of illicit drug use and its consequences, and who must see it in its many dimensions, know that if we are to be effective, our responses must be thoughtful, comprehensive, balanced, and effective.

By comparison, some solutions that have been put forward to resolve the problem of drugs, and crime, and violence, seem remarkably simple. And plausible. Until they are forced into the bright light of day.

This is what I want to talk about: simple solutions, tough problems,

Lee P. Brown, "Eight Myths About Drugs: There Are No Simple Solutions," a speech given at the Drug Policy Reform Conference of the Civil Liberties Union of Massachusetts, May 21, 1994.

difficult choices.

From time to time one hears some remarkable—even bizarre—assertions by so-called drug experts about what the drug situation is. The purported solutions then follow the mythology.

Eight myths about drugs

Let me outline what I have come to call *Eight Myths about Drugs.* These can be put in straightforward terms.

The first myth is that everything is getting worse, and that nothing is getting better. It follows from this that the so-called drug war is a failure, and that we should abandon it in favor of another approach.

In fact, drug use data from the nation's households and secondary schools show substantial declines in overall drug use over the past decade:

- In 1979, more than 23 million Americans used some illicit drug. By 1992 the number had dropped to 11.4 million.
- Past month cocaine use, which peaked in 1985 at 8.6 million users, had dropped to 1.3 million users by 1992. This was accompanied by a similarly dramatic decline in the use of cocaine by adolescents from the mid-1980s until 1992.
- We have a severe, continuing problem with the chronic, hard-core, addicted use of drugs. We freely acknowledge this; indeed, we want this to be broadly known. The nation's estimated 2.7 million hard-core users are our most serious concern. They cause the most damage to themselves, to their families, and to their communities. They are the most important single focus of our National Drug Control Strategy.
- As troubling, we have indicators of recent increases in the use of drugs by secondary school children.
- Overall, the country—not the government, not a particular Administration, but the country—has experienced major declines in non-addictive, casual use of illicit drugs. The number of users of any illicit drugs today is the same level as it was in the early 1970s.

Let us reason about this: Can this really be called failure?

Now, it is sometimes alleged that one can't trust what the government data says.

In fact, the government does not collect the data. The Research Triangle Institute, an independent nongovernment organization, conducts the Household Survey. The University of Michigan's Institute for Social Research conducts the survey of drug use in the nations's secondary schools.

A second myth is that current policy—one suspects any current policy—is making things worse. This myth says that current drug policy does not address the real problems, which are violence and HIV [human immunodeficiency virus] transmission.

In fact, violence and HIV transmission are only part of the human carnage that results from drug use. Addiction, drug-exposed infants, drug-induced accidents, loss of productivity, loss of employment, family breakdown, and the degeneration of communities are others. All directly flow from drug use itself. As the number of users increases, these problems will multiply.

Current policy directly addresses these issues through specific strategies to prevent new use, to effectively treat hard-core users, and to bring overwhelming force against the street markets.

A third myth is that enforcement just adds to the problem. Drug enforcement and the application of criminal justice should be given up in favor of harm reduction approaches.

In fact, effective enforcement serves to reduce drug supply, drive up prices, reduce the number of users, and decrease the effects of chronic hard-core use. There is a demonstrable *inverse* relationship between the price of cocaine and the number of individuals seeking emergency room treatment. The criminal justice system, moreover, provides means to remand drug offenders to effective treatment.

A fourth myth is that there is massive support for policy change by social thinkers, policy-level officials, and the public at large. This includes broad support for legalization, or the decriminalization of drug use.

In fact, there is no massive support for legalization. A 1990 Gallup poll showed that 80 percent of the public thought that legalizing drugs was a bad idea. Only 14 percent thought that it was a good idea. Among American twelfth-graders surveyed in the 1992–93 school year, 84 percent said that their friends would disapprove of their smoking marijuana regularly; *94 percent* said that their friends would disapprove of their taking cocaine occasionally.

Reflecting the views of the American public, there is no meaningful support within Congress for the legalization of illicit drugs.

And *in fact,* policy-level officials who are directly responsible for the drug issue—*beginning with the President*—oppose legalization. I do, too.

A fifth myth is that legalizing drugs, or decriminalizing drug use, will eliminate the illegal drug markets and the violence in our streets.

I do not dispute that drug markets do, in fact, generate violence. But the way to deal with the markets and the associated violence is to dry up the pool of users through effective prevention and treatment, and through the use of street enforcement, as many communities throughout the country are now struggling to do.

A 1990 Gallup poll showed that 80 percent of the public thought that legalizing drugs was a bad idea.

A sixth myth is that legalizing drugs will be free of cost. As *this* myth goes, there is nothing to suggest that legalizing drugs will increase drug use, or its consequences.

In fact, the suggestion that legalizing drugs will not increase drug use is a fantastic myth.

Our own national experience with Prohibition is indicative of what would happen if drug laws and drug enforcement were eliminated. Alcohol use data from the 1930s shows clearly that the repeal of the Volstead Act resulted in an immediate, sustained rise in the use of alcohol to levels higher than those that existed prior to Prohibition.

We believe that the repeal of drug control laws would, likewise, result in an immediate, sustained rise in the use of drugs—and a concomitant rise in the casualties of the use of drugs.

Another, seventh, myth is that there are excellent foreign models to show that decriminalization works: The Netherlands and the U.K. are two.

This is another fantastic myth. One need only read the international press to realize the degree to which the Dutch have visited upon themselves misery from drug abuse by enacting drug laws that go unenforced, and policies that encourage "responsible" use rather than discourage any use at all. The Dutch are pleased to say they have remained mostly unscathed by drug use by their own citizens. They cannot say the same of the many thousands of foreign visitors who arrive to buy drugs, steal or panhandle to keep using them, and then ask the Dutch to treat them for addiction.

And one need only recall the disastrous experience of Great Britain with the controlled distribution of heroin. In the years between 1959 and 1968, according to the 1981 *British Medical Journal*, the number of heroin addicts in the U.K. *doubled* every sixteen months. The experiment was, of course, terminated. But addiction rates in the U.K. have not subsided.

Given what we have to do to address the terrible consequences of drug use, legalization is a marginal issue.

At the same time, no one mentions Italy, which permits heroin and other drugs to be used legally, and where the number of heroin addicts—some 350,000, by official estimates—and the level of HIV prevalence—an estimated 70 percent—are higher than those in any other country in Western Europe. I ask myself at times why those who advocate drug policy reform are so quiet about the Italian model.

And then there is a final, eighth myth. This one says that drug use is a personal matter, and that it affects no one other than the user.

There's no good thing to say about this. Given what we know about the effects of drugs, this is simply wrong. No one familiar with alcohol abuse would suggest that alcoholism affects the user only. And no one who works with the drug-addicted would tell you that their use of drugs has not affected others—usually families and friends in the first instance.

Through this day, you have heard a number of views about the so-called war on drugs and what it supposedly does or does not do. Let me make a simple point, now: *The war analogy is false.* We in the Clinton Administration do not use this term to describe the long, difficult struggle to free Americans from the grip of use and addiction. We do not make "war" on the American people. And we do not find useful a concept that suggests a beginning and an end to this struggle, with "victory" as the goal.

No doubt it is helpful to some to use the war terminology as a straw man. But the reality of drug use, and the policies that must address the problem, are very different, and I suggest that it is time to recognize the reality rather than the mythology—here, as well as with the other myths that I have mentioned.

Let me conclude with a few overall points.

First, *given what the overwhelming number of Americans want, and given what we have to do to address the terrible consequences of drug use, legaliza-*

tion is a marginal issue. It does not get to the core of the problem. In seeking to satisfy the few, it subverts the best interests of the many. In purporting to provide a quick, simple, costless cure for crime and violence in America, it fails to suggest how *more* drug availability will not lead to *more* drug use—and more devastating consequences.

It does not deal with the essential business of responsible policy-making:

- *How* to provide effective prevention education for adolescents;
- *How* to make effective treatment available for our estimated 2.7 million hard-core drug users;
- *How* to develop effective workplace strategies that reduce accidents, reduce employer's health care costs, and improve productivity;
- *How* to ensure that health care reform provides for those in need of treatment.

And it does not deal with the essential business of bringing together health policy and criminal justice policy, to improve society as a whole.

This is the real story: the day-in-day-out, blood and guts of policy-making that deals directly with the very complex issues of human behavior, that recognizes that there are no simple solutions.

In 1917, the renowned American journalist and social observer, H.L. Mencken, remarked: "There is always an easy solution to every human problem—neat, plausible, and wrong."

To the overwhelming number of Americans, to the Clinton Administration, to the American Congress, to American policy makers of this as well as prior Administrations, to Americans involved with drug programs across the country, to Americans in drug-blighted communities across the country, legalization is exactly such a solution—neat, plausible, and wrong.

Speaking for these Americans and for this Administration, I can tell you that *it's just not going to happen.*

What we need to do is to get on with the business of reducing drug availability, preventing drug use, treating addicts, of restoring the value of the American family—in short, of addressing some of the most basic and pressing issues of the country.

I invite those who seek policy reform to light a candle and stop cursing the dark. Come in out of the cold, work with us on these problems—help us find realistic and meaningful solutions to drug use and its devastating effects on millions of our citizens.

Let us get on with the serious business of drug policy, together.

Organizations to Contact

The editors have compiled the following list of organizations concerned with the issues debated in this book. The descriptions are derived from materials provided by the organizations. All have publications or information available for interested readers. The list was compiled on the date of publication of the present volume; names, addresses, and phone numbers may change. Be aware that many organizations take several weeks or longer to respond to inquiries, so allow as much time as possible.

American Civil Liberties Union (ACLU)
132 W. 43rd St.
New York, NY 10036
(212) 944-9800

The ACLU, one of the oldest civil liberties organizations in the United States, favors decriminalization of drugs. It opposes indiscriminate drug testing as a violation of the right to privacy. The ACLU publishes information packets on drug legalization and decriminalization.

Canadian Foundation for Drug Policy (CFDP)
(613) 238-5909
fax: (613) 238-2891
e-mail: eoscapel@fox.nstn.ca
Web site: http:/fox.nstn.ca/~eoscapel/cfdp/dfdp.html

Founded by several of Canada's leading drug policy specialists, CFDP is a non-profit organization that examines the objectives and consequences of Canada's drug laws and policies. When necessary, the foundation recommends alternatives that it believes would make Canada's drug policies more effective and humane. CFDP discusses drug policy issues with the Canadian government, media, and general public. It also disseminates educational materials.

Cato Institute
1000 Massachusetts Ave. NW
Washington, DC 20001-5403
(202) 842-0200

The institute is a public policy research foundation dedicated to limiting the control of government and to protecting individual liberty. It studies the problem of drug abuse and strongly favors drug legalization. It publishes the *Cato Journal* three times a year and the *Cato Policy Report* bimonthly.

Council on Drug Abuse (CODA)
16 Scarlett Rd.
Toronto, ON M6N 4K1
CANADA
(416) 763-1491
fax: (416) 763-5343

CODA studies the misuse and abuse of all types of drugs. It analyzes the harmful effects of drugs on society and supports public education concerning the causes, effects, prevention, and cure of all forms of drug dependency. CODA produces educational materials related to drug abuse issues.

Drug Enforcement Administration (DEA)
700 Army Navy Dr.
Arlington, VA 22202
(202) 307-1000

The DEA is the federal agency charged with enforcing the nation's drug laws. The agency concentrates on stopping narcotics smuggling and distribution organizations in the United States and abroad. It publishes *Drug Enforcement Magazine* three times a year.

Drug Policy Foundation (DPF)
4455 Connecticut Ave. NW, Suite B-500
Washington, DC 20008-2302
(202) 537-5005

The Drug Policy Foundation is an independent, nonprofit think tank founded in 1986 that promotes alternatives to the drug war. DPF believes that drug prohibition has failed and that a more rational system of drug control is needed. The foundation represents a range of reform ideas—from allowing medical access to banned drugs to legalization for adults. It publishes the bimonthly *Drug Policy Letter* and the book *The Great Drug War*. It also distributes *Press Clips*, an annual compilation of newspaper articles on drug legalization issues.

The Heritage Foundation
214 Massachusetts Ave. NE
Washington, DC 20002
(202) 546-4400

The Heritage Foundation is a conservative public policy research institute that opposes the legalization of drugs and advocates strengthening law enforcement to stop drug abuse. It publishes position papers on a broad range of topics, including drug issues. Its regular publications include the monthly *Policy Review*, the *Backgrounder* series of occasional papers, and the Heritage Lectures series.

International Narcotic Enforcement Officers Association (INEOA)
112 State St., Suite 1200
Albany, NY 12207
(518) 463-6232

INEOA examines national and international narcotics laws and seeks ways to improve those laws in order to prevent drug abuse. It also studies law enforcement methods to find the most effective ways to reduce illegal drug use. The association publishes *International Drug Report* and *Narc Officer*, both monthly journals, and a newsletter devoted to drug control.

Libertarian Party
1528 Pennsylvania Ave. SE
Washington, DC 20003-3116
(202) 543-1988

The Libertarian Party is a political party whose goal is to ensure respect for individual rights and liberties. It advocates the repeal of all laws prohibiting the production, sale, possession, or use of drugs. The party believes law enforcement should focus on preventing violent crimes against persons and property rather than on prosecuting people who use drugs. It publishes the bimonthly *Libertarian Party News* and periodic *Issues Papers* and distributes a compilation of articles supporting drug legalization.

National Clearinghouse for Alcohol and Drug Information (NCADI)
PO Box 2345
Rockville, MD 20847-2345
(800) 729-6686

NCADI is an information service of the Office for Substance Abuse Prevention of the U.S. Department of Health and Human Services. The clearinghouse provides free alcohol and drug prevention and education materials, including technical reports, pamphlets, and posters. It publishes a bimonthly newsletter, *Prevention Pipeline: An Alcohol and Drug Awareness Service*, containing the latest available research, resources, and activities in the prevention field.

National Institute of Justice (NIJ)
PO Box 6000
Rockville, MD 20852
(800) 851-4320

The institute serves as a clearinghouse for information on the causes, prevention, and control of crime. Among the publications available from it are *Probing the Links Between Drugs and Crime* and pamphlets on drug-free work environments, on drug legalization, and on specific drugs.

National Organization for the Reform of Marijuana Laws (NORML)
1001 Connecticut Ave. NW, Suite 1010
Washington, DC 20036
(202) 483-5500

NORML fights to legalize marijuana and to help those who have been convicted and sentenced for processing or selling marijuana. It publishes the newsletter *Active Resistance*, published five to six times per year, as well as the monthly newsletters *Ongoing Briefing* and *Potpourri*.

Parents Against Drugs (PAD)
7 Hawksdale Rd.
North York, ON M3K 1W3
CANADA

Parents Against Drugs provides educational materials and support to families concerned about alcohol and drug abuse. It seeks to educate parents, teachers, young people, and the general public about drug abuse prevention. The organization publishes the *PAD Newsletter* three times a year.

Bibliography

Books

Ronald Bayer and Gerald Oppenheimer, eds. — *Confronting Drug Policy: Illicit Drugs in a Free Society.* New York: Cambridge University Press, 1993.

Daniel K. Benjamin and Roger LeRoy Miller — *Undoing Drugs: Beyond Legalization.* New York: Basic Books, 1991.

Elliott Currie — *Reckoning: Drugs, the Cities, and the American Future.* New York: Hill & Wang, 1993.

Steven B. Duke and Albert C. Gross — *America's Longest War: Rethinking Our Tragic Crusade Against Drugs.* New York: Jeremy P. Tarcher/Putnam Books, 1993.

Jeffrey A. Eisenach — *Winning the Drug War: New Challenges for the 1990s.* Washington, DC: Heritage Foundation, 1991.

Jeffrey M. Elliot — *Drugs and American Society.* Boston: Allyn & Bacon, 1994.

Rod L. Evans and Irwin M. Berent — *Drug Legalization: For and Against.* Peru, IL: Open Court Publishing, 1992.

Mathea Falco — *The Making of a Drug-Free America.* New York: Random House, 1992.

Douglas N. Husak — *Drugs and Rights.* New York: Cambridge University Press, 1992.

Sam Staley — *Drug Policy and the Decline of American Cities.* New Brunswick, NJ: Transaction Publishers, 1992.

Harold T. Traver and Mark S. Gaylord — *Drugs, Law, and the State.* New Brunswick, NJ: Transaction Publishers, 1992.

Arnold S. Trebach and James A. Inciardi — *Legalize It? Debating American Drug Policy.* Washington, DC: American University Press, 1993.

Periodicals

Doug Bandow — "Sometimes Marijuana Is the Best Medicine," *Wall Street Journal,* January 28, 1993.

William J. Bennett — "Should Drugs Be Legalized?" *Reader's Digest,* March 1990.

William J. Bennett and John P. Walters — "Drugs: Face the Facts, Focus on Education," *Insight,* March 6, 1995. Available from 3600 New York Ave. NE, Washington, DC 20002.

Cynthia Cotts — "Legal Eagles," *Village Voice,* December 21, 1993. Available from 36 Cooper Square, New York, NY 10003.

CQ Researcher	"Treating Addiction," January 6, 1995. Available from 1414 22nd St. NW, Washington, DC 20037.
Elliott Currie	"The Limits of Legalization," *American Prospect*, Winter 1992. Available from 146 Mt. Auburn St., Cambridge, MA 02138.
Ed D'Angelo	"The Moral Culture of Drug Prohibition," *Humanist*, September/October 1994. Available from PO Box 1188, Amherst, NY 14226-7188.
Midge Decter	"Who Is Addicted to What?" *Commentary*, April 1994.
Richard J. Dennis	"The Economics of Legalizing Drugs," *Atlantic Monthly*, November 1990.
Jefferson Fish	"Discontinuous Change and the War on Drugs," *Humanist*, September/October 1994.
Thomas P. Griesa	"There Is No Case for Legalizing Drugs," *Wall Street Journal*, August 10, 1993.
Joseph P. Kane	"The Challenge of Legalizing Drugs," *America*, August 8, 1992.
Herbert D. Kleber	"Our Current Approach to Drug Abuse—Progress, Problems, Proposals," *New England Journal of Medicine*, February 3, 1994. Available from 10 Shattuck St., Boston, MA 02115-6094.
Ethan A. Nadelmann	"America's Drug Problem: The Case for Legalization," *Dissent*, Spring 1992.
James Ostrowski	"War on Drugs, War on Progress," *Liberty*, September 1992. Available from 1532 Sims Way #1, Port Townsend, WA 98368.
Daniel M. Perrine	"The View from Platform Zero: How Holland Handles Its Drug Problem," *America*, October 15, 1994.
A.M. Rosenthal	"Surrender on Drugs?" *New York Times*, December 10, 1993.
Michael Ruby	"Should Drugs Be Legalized?" *U.S. News & World Report*, December 20, 1993.
Chi Chi Sileo	"Is It Time to Just Say No to the War on Drugs?" *Insight*, February 7, 1994.
Eric Sterling	"What Should We Do About Drugs? Manage the Problem Through Legalization," *Vital Speeches of the Day*, August 1, 1991.
Jacob Sullum	"Selling Pot," *Reason*, June 1993. Available from 3415 S. Sepulveda Blvd., Suite 400, Los Angeles, CA 90034.

Index